SOPAS

A brief history of Portuguese islanders,
the Cape Cod town of Falmouth,
and the Feast of the Holy Ghost

by

LEWIS A. WHITE

Amerazor Publishing Company

Library of Congress Catalog Number: TBD

ISBN-: 0983732000

EAN: 978-0-9837320-0-6

Published by Amerazor Publishing Company, Falmouth, MA

Printed in the United States of America

Dedication

To all hard working members of Holy Ghost Societies everywhere
who are no longer with us.
They were faithful to their traditions and to each other.
No one exemplified this more than Frank M. Teixeira,
a faithful member for over eighty years
who died on Pentecost Sunday 2010,
literally while sopas was being freely given to anyone
who came to the Fresh Pond Holy Ghost Hall.

Preface

This book is about the experience of Portuguese islanders in Falmouth, Massachusetts who left their homeland in the late nineteenth and twentieth centuries. It is the story of twelve founding families, two waves of immigration half a century apart, three societies, and a continuing religious folk tradition firmly rooted in the thirteenth century.

The founders of the Festa do Divino Espirito Santo in Fresh Pond[1] referred to their organization as the Holy Ghost Society. This literal English translation may bring to mind movie and television images of earthbound spirits, psychics, mediums, and such, but in many Christian religions the phrase Holy Ghost, or Holy Spirit, is a specific reference to the third person of the Holy Trinity. Over 14 million Catholics in America attend a weekly Mass[2] that includes the phrase "I believe in the Holy Spirit..." This belief is at the very heart of a religious folk tradition that originated in Europe and spread westward, crossing the Atlantic to the Azores and other Portuguese islands, and from there to the Americas.

---

1   This book uses "Fresh Pond" to describe an area near the smaller of two ponds in Falmouth, Massachusetts, with that name. It is between Smallville and Waquoit, both parts of what is sometimes called East Falmouth.

2   The Center for Applied Research in the Apostolate (http//:cara.georgetown.edu) estimates that 22% of the 65 million Roman Catholics in the United States attend Mass every Sunday.

The focal point of the festa is the serving of a unique meal called sopas, free of charge, to anyone who shows up at the annual festival. This tradition continues to this day in hundreds of communities in the United States, Brazil, and Portuguese islands; each has evolved over the years and, if you will forgive the pun, each has its unique flavor.

Table of Contents

Acknowledgements

First, my thanks to the many elders who have freely shared their memories, records, and photographs, especially:

- Elsie Teixeira, daughter of founder Antone Souza. Now deceased.
- Ethyl Sylvia, granddaughter of founder Manuel Viera Martins ("Ti Calhau"). Now deceased.
- Kathleen Rose (Santiago) DePonte, granddaughter of Francisco Teixeira. Now deceased.
- Clara "Nini" Ferreira, granddaughter of founder Francisco Perry Da Rosa.
- Elsie May (Teixeira) Mello, granddaughter of founder Francisco Teixeira. Now deceased.
- Ed "Sparky" Santiago, grandson of founder Francisco Teixeira.
- Milton Lawrence Servis, grandson of founder Joseph Silveira Andrews ("Tio Carassa").

Second, my thanks to current members of the Fresh Pond Holy Ghost Society who have also shared their memories and records, especially Billy Valadao, the current President, and his first lady Olivia who provided most of the actual festa recipes. And to members of the Irmandade do Divino Espirito Santo of East Falmouth, especially Tony Fernandes.

And to members of the Falmouth Portuguese-American Association, especially Joaquim Lima, Joe Martinho, Ginny Rosa, and John Sylvia.

Third, the Falmouth Historical Society, Carney Library (Ferreira-Mendes Archives, University of Massachusetts-Dartmouth), and New Bedford Public Library for their too often thankless task of collecting, preserving, and indexing materials that may someday be of use, especially the tireless efforts of archivists Mary Sicchio, Sofia Pacheco, and Paul Cyr for guiding me through them.

Fourth, to my valued friend and historian, Jim Gould, who shared genealogical information relevant to this book.

Fifth, my merciless editors:

- Sandy Freitas, a paralegal and extraordinarily meticulous editor.
- Susan Haynes, my younger sister and past President of the Sisters of the Holy Ghost, for her content review.
- David Sanders, an exceptionally comprehensive editor who suggested phrasing, structural, and organizational improvements.

Sixth, my daughter Julianna Marie White, who documented years of feast preparation and celebration in hundreds of photographs to help me with this book.

Seventh, to my wife Amelia Leontire for her patience, support, graciousness, and encouragement, especially in focusing on completion.

To all these people, and to my relatives, friends, and neighbors who tolerated my inattention while I obsessed writing this book, my heartfelt appreciation.

The cow in the street

While I was growing up, the Holy Ghost Hall was usually a quiet place. It was "kitty corner" across the street from our home. Sometimes my brother and I would sneak over there to climb the stone arch in front of the hall, starting simultaneously at the opposite ends in a race, scrambling over each other at the top to get to the other side. We were too young to believe it was dangerous – but smart enough not to tell our parents.

When you are very young, many things make you curious. For me, sixty years ago, one of them was the sight of a lone farmer in *clean* coveralls walking down the street past our house, leading a cow on a rope. We lived in the country, but cows were supposed to be in the fields or in a barn, not walking down the street. They strolled past on their way to the back of the Holy Ghost Hall; I never saw the cow again. That evening my father said it meant the annual Feast of the Holy Ghost would be held in three days[3].

The feast, or festa as the old timers called it, was a glorious event eagerly anticipated by everyone in the community. For my great grandparents, it was the biggest event of the year, continuing a tradition from their own childhoods in Pico and São Miguel, two of the nine Azores islands of Portugal. In those days (the early nineteen fifties), the festa began with a parade starting half a mile away with young girls in banana curls and crisp white dresses on a float, one girl holding a very old crown, and a procession of old timers, followed by an old fashioned Portuguese marching band, all going past our house to the hall. The feast seemed to "officially" start with the exuberant arrival of the parade.

Traditionally the band played for their meal, so after playing one more song in front of the hall, they ate first. After eating their fill, they went to the outdoor bandstand and played while the members of the Holy Ghost Society ate next. Everyone else lined up for the free food served inside the building: plates heaping with coarse bread soaked in a beef broth, some mint, a piece of the tenderest meat imaginable – plus, with a little luck, the best tasting

---

3   Traditionally the Festa is on Pentecost Sunday, and the cow was slaughtered three days before.

cabbage ever. It was "all you could eat," and so people did – and in a time when people sometimes put pieces of cardboard in the bottom of their shoes to cover the holes, "all you could eat" was a *really* big deal.

Afterwards, there was more live music, dancing, and merriment. Ice cream cones that our grandfather served us for free (later I learned that meant he paid, not us). And there would be soda. A crazy auction took place where people paid outrageous prices, teased each other to pay even more, and laughed about it. So many people of all ages gathered to share stories, all of them happy. Wonderful memories!

✳ ✳ ✳

More than fifty years, two marriages, seven relocations, and two careers later, I looked up from the work piled on my desk to see an old family friend - Sparky Santiago – walk into my office sporting the contagious smile that defines him. My parents had both died the previous year, within four months of each other, after sixty years of marriage. Sparky had known my father since childhood, and his sister Kathleen and my mother were best friends. I had not seen him since the funerals.

Following tradition, my brother and sisters and I had decided to donate the meat for the festa that year in our parents' honor. As head cook of the feast, I assumed Sparky was there to thank us for the donation. He was, but there was much more to his visit than just that.

"Louie," he began. Louie — no one called me that any-more. My deceased parents, of course, and my siblings, and a few childhood friends, but nowadays it was Lew or Lewis or (to some employees, customers, and colleagues) Mr. White, or to poker buddies, "Big Lew." Louie was the name of the long deceased uncle I was named after, another of Sparky's childhood friends. "Louie" ?

"Louie, your father cooked for us, you know. And your grandfather helped before him. And your great grandfather before your grandfather. You know, they all helped. Now they are all gone and you're the oldest son; the way I see it, it's your turn."

I knew nothing about the festas except the eating, drinking, music, and auction. Most of my life had been lived in other parts of the country, and I had only returned to the area a few years before. I had never even joined the Holy Ghost Society.

WHAT WAS HE THINKING?

Sitting in my high back leather executive chair looking across a polished seven foot cherry desk, I was initially mildly amused, but as the seconds began quietly ticking away in silence, memories of my ancestors surfaced and I found myself actually considering what he had asked; the idea of helping cook the meat we had donated in my parent's memory took root, flourished, and ultimately overwhelmed me. Much to my surprise, I heard a firm voice remarkably like mine saying, "Of course, of course. I'd be honored. Thank you, thank you, for asking."

WHAT WAS I THINKING?

That was in 2008, four feasts ago. I have been cooking ever since.

In 2001, I visited the Azores with my father, and found the islands an absolute delight. With the bright blue Atlantic framing almost every vista, rolling hills, rugged coastline, patchwork farms, whitewashed houses with red tile roofs, the islands are incredibly beautiful. The climate is wonderfully moderate, much like San Francisco. Separated from Europe by 850 miles of ocean, the air is remarkably clean. The food is delicious, fresh, and often uniquely prepared, most of it locally grown or caught offshore. There were more cows than people. São Miguel seemed like one huge well-manicured garden, dotted with picturesque towns. And the people were unusually friendly, helpful, and scrupulously honest.

During a conversation at the next festa with Frank Teixeira, I asked him if his father had ever returned to the Azores. Frank smiled and said he asked him that once, and old Francisco practically spat his answer back with a scornful "go back to what?" I was so enamoured of the Azores that I was truly stunned, and wondered why they left, under what conditions — and why did they come here?

Sparky's visit reconnected me to my heritage and rekindled the curiosity aroused seven years before by immigrant Francisco Teixeira's vehement answer to his son's question. This book is the result of trying to satisfy that curiosity and to share what I found with others.

The Cauldron

THE AZORES

The Azores are an archipelago of nine islands and eight formigas[4] spread across 400 miles of ocean about 850 miles from Portugal. They were uninhabited until 1432, when immigrants from Portugal, as well as from France, England, and other countries began settling there.

Today there are far more people of Azorean descent in America than there are in the Azores. Most of them are in California, Massachusetts, Rhode Island, Hawaii, New Jersey, and Florida. As with many other cultures, these people with a common language and shared cultural traditions tended to settle in the same communities. They formed fraternal organizations to help each other and to continue their traditions in America.

---

4   Outcroppings of rocks, remnants of volcanic eruptions. Literally translates to English as "ants". Some call them islets.

The Festa do Divino Espirito Santo (Feast of the Holy Spirit[5]) is the most widely known[6] of these traditions. The largest organization is the Irmandade do Divino Espirito Santo (I.D.E.S.), with 57 groups in the United States. Most are in California; there are only three in Massachusetts.

Most Massachusetts-based groups are independent of the I.D.E.S., including the Fresh Pond Holy Ghost Society.[7]. It is one of the oldest groups in the United States, with roots in the 1890s before the organization had even constructed a hall. Its founders were from the first and second waves of immigrants, and their descendants still celebrate on the traditional Pentecost[8] Sunday as was done in their villages in the Azores of the 1890s. Descendants of the third wave of immigration also celebrate with a feast a few weeks later. While the two festas are essentially similar, differences exist (including preparation of the broth and the type of bread used) because the original group maintains the traditions of the 1890s while the newer group reflects the newer traditions of the Azores in the 1960s and 1970s.

The Fresh Pond Holy Ghost Society is small compared to other similar groups. Their hall is located in an area of Falmouth labeled Smalltown[9] on some maps (including mapquest.com and the U.S. Geodetic Survey). A century

---

5   The Holy Spirit is often symbolized as a dove. In the bible, John 2:32 describes the baptism of Jesus in the river Jordan by Saint John the Baptist. When Jesus came out of the water, John the Baptist saw the Spirit of God descending upon Him from heaven like a dove."

6   Googling "Festa do Divino Espirito Santo" resulted in 320,000 hits on the Internet. A search for "Holy Ghost Society" returned over twice that many.

7   Records use various terms to mean the same organization, e.g., Waquoit Holy Ghost Association, Fresh Pond Holy Ghost Society, and so forth. This book will generally use Fresh Pond Holy Ghost Society.

8   Seven weeks after Easter.

9   Not for its size, though, but after a prominent family in the area.

ago it was referred to as "Calico Town" because of the colorful clothing worn by people living there, in sharp contrast to what was then worn by the more staid New Englanders.

This is their story.

FALMOUTH

Originally called Sucannesset, Falmouth occupies about forty-six square miles on the southwestern triangular tip of Cape Cod [10]. It includes the villages of Falmouth, East Falmouth, West Falmouth, North Falmouth, Woods Hole, Waquoit, Hatchville[11], and Teaticket. Falmouth has forty ponds and almost seventy miles of shoreline — including twelve miles of public beaches.

Its relatively cool summertime breezes, proximity to Martha's Vineyard and Nantucket, and endless boating opportunities make it a premier summer tourist destination. In the early days, though, it was primarily a fishing and farming community.

For untold centuries, Native Americans[12] visited Falmouth and lived year round in the Waquoit area because of its fresh water, rivers, sheltered bay, and hardwood and jack pine forest. The rivers had perch and two kinds of herring (alewife and blueback). The bay with its

---

10   Cape Cod as defined in the English charter of April 10, 1606 to the original Plymouth Company, superseded by the 1620 charter.

11   Known until the late nineteenth century as "East End" (of Falmouth)

12   Except for occasional incursions by the Narragansetts, the Wampanoag tribe. Before Europeans arrived, there were about 8,000 Wampanoag Indians in about 40 villages between what is today Rhode Island and Provincetown. European epidemics reduced this to about 1,000 by 1675. Only 400 survived King Philip's war. Massachusetts ended tribal status in 1870 but the descendants organized the Wampanoag Nation in 1928. Today there are five groups in Assonet, Gay Head, Herring Pond, Mashpee, and Namasket.

barrier beach and small estuary was teeming with fish and shellfish, and the forest supplied plenty of deer and other wildlife. The environment contained edible and medicinal plants that supplemented the corn grown by the Indians. Native Americans frequented Falmouth in the spring, summer, and fall for similar reasons; there is ample evidence of temporary camps but none of permanent ones.

OUTCASTS

Falmouth was settled in 1661 by outcasts from Barnstable seeking religious tolerance. Barnstable was founded by a minister[13] who had originally settled in Plymouth

---

13   Reverend John Lothrop, a former pastor of a Congregational Church in London. He arrived in Boston in 1634.

after being imprisoned in England and then banished to America after completing his sentence.[14] He later moved to Hingham, where he served for a few years as a pastor before his church split, which drove him to establish a new community in Barnstable. One of the minister's original followers[15], after years of service, was judged a sympathizer with the Quakers in Sandwich and was, for that reason, stripped of his civil employment and removed from the list of freemen. He and others suffering similar intolerance, left to form Sucannessct — later renamed Falmouth.

At first Falmouth's farms were very productive. The rich topsoil accumulated from centuries of forest decomposition proved extremely fertile for a few generations of farmers. However, unlike their European homelands, underlying that thin layer of topsoil was the Cape's base of clay. Widespread deforestation exposed the nutrient rich soil to Cape Cod's wind and rain; much of it blew away, washed away, or was overrun with sand unleashed after their animals foraged on the grassy sand dunes. Overuse of the soil without sufficient replenishment took its toll. America's westward expansion made new farmland elsewhere more attractive. Settlers had cleared the hardwood and jack pine forest for farmland and homes, and when the soil was no longer viable, the land was largely abandoned to the twisted, gnarly, low trees of scrub oak and pitch pine that dominate the Cape to this day.

Falmouth also prospered through fishing, coastal shipping, and small-scale manufacturing. Local forests temporarily provided an ample supply of firewood, not only

---

14   Plymouth was founded by Pilgrims fleeing Leiden in the Netherlands, where the British pursued them after the Pilgrims left England.

15   Isaac Robinson, who was born ether in Amsterdam or Leiden about 1610, shipped to Boston in 1630, and lived in Plymouth before moving to Scituate, leaving to found Barnstable with Rev. Lothrop.

within Falmouth but also for shipping to Nantucket and Martha's Vineyard. The town had a minor but significant role in whaling, especially when the industry was dominated by Nantucket. Shipbuilding was a natural adjunct to both coastal shipping and whaling. Falmouth's shoreline made salt production initially very productive. The Pacific Guano Factory was established in Woods Hole, where Pacific island guano, Chilean nitrates, Sicilian brimstone, and German potash were mixed with oil from locally caught menhaden to make fertilizer.

EAST FALMOUTH, FRESH POND AND WAQUOIT

Falmouth's original eastern boundary was the Coonamesset River. Mashpee's western boundary was then the Child's River. The land between the Coonamesset and Childs rivers was not part of either settlement. As Falmouth prospered, community leaders were granted permission to purchase additional land from Native Americans, and in 1685 they purchased the land between the Coonamesset and Childs rivers. This area became known as East Falmouth; Fresh Pond was about a quarter mile from the Mashpee border. Waquoit was then part of Mashpee.

Waquoit was largely defined by water: the Quashnet River to the west, Waquoit Bay to the south, the Childs River to the east, and what would become the Sandwich town line to the north.

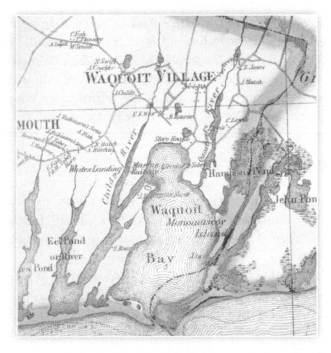

In the 1880 Barnstable County atlas, a separate breakout was needed for Waquoit and East Falmouth, but not for sparsely populated Fresh Pond.

Waquoit flourished as an agricultural, fishing, and whaling community, and its rivers were dammed to create small local mills for processing wool, wood, and grains. Waterpower was used for a yarn mill and a saw/grist mill, with offices and other company buildings nearby; it also attracted a wagon and barrel factory. Boats were built and maintained at the mouth of the Childs River, which offered a harbor deep enough for shipbuilding and transporting goods by water. Many sea captains built their residences there, and then established local businesses when they retired. By the early 1800s, it was an important

economic contributor to the town. In 1841, Falmouth annexed Waquoit, including all land from the Childs River
to Red Brook. This is why, paradoxically, East Falmouth is
not the easternmost part of Falmouth. Further confusing in
some old references is the use of the term Upper Waquoit
to refer to Fresh Pond and parts of East Falmouth.

AN ECONOMY IN FLUX

Less than a half century later, Waquoit's economy was in
trouble: crops were down, the railroad along Buzzard's
Bay weakened local businesses, and shipbuilding was in
decline[16].

The Pacific Guano Company was a catalyst for Waquoit's
economic decline: it induced the Old Colony Railroad to
extend a line to Woods Hole. Fresh Pond and Waquoit are
on the *easternmost* part of Falmouth; the railroad came to
Falmouth following the seacoast on the *west* side. Stations
were built in North Falmouth, West Falmouth, Falmouth,
and Woods Hole. This favored economic growth in those
areas, both residential and commercial, to the detriment
of East Falmouth and Waquoit. More reliable, timely,
and cheaper transportation opened up local businesses to
more distant competitors with better natural resources and
cheaper labor. Larger, more efficient mills like those of
New Bedford and Fall River devalued the small mills in
Waquoit and East Falmouth, which were eventually abandoned. The yarn mill in Waquoit burned down in 1894, for
example, and was never rebuilt. One of the factory houses

---

16   The Town of Falmouth also suffered from the failures of the Pacific Guano
Company, which employed about 200 workers, as well as the dying off of the salt works
that dotted the ocean shore.

was sold and known for a while as "Riverside Cottage," a place frequented by fishermen[17] eager to hook the "salter" trout in Quashnet River.

Whaling was another factor that contributed to the community's economic decline. In the early days of colonial whaling Falmouth played a significant but quickly diminished role in shipbuilding[18] as the industry focus shifted from Nantucket to New Bedford. The whaling industry had been in decline since the discovery of oil refining and the profitable development of oil wells. Falmouth suffered as the infrastructure to support whaling dissipated, and underutilized New Bedford maritime resources sought smaller scale work that might previously have gone to Falmouth.

When the railroad came to town, they built a new railroad terminal in Woods Hole. It had eleven railroad spurs to handle shipping, making it a far more attractive port than Waquoit for goods moved by water. These combined factors meant less shipbuilding and maintenance at Waquoit, and less commercial water traffic[19].

Fishing, especially shellfishing, would remain profitable for years and provided a good income for many hard working individuals but was never a major economic factor. The same was true for small scale food farming, but the flocks of Falmouth's Merino sheep that once provided the wool for Waquoit's yarn mills would largely disappear because of the depleted soil, crash in wool prices, and, to

---

17   Including people like Daniel Webster

18   From 1812-1865, more than a hundred ships varying in size up to 400 tons were built in Falmouth.

19   Falmouth created its inner harbor from Deacon's Pond in 1908.

some degree, Falmouth ordinances favoring road traffic over sheep grazing[20].

Falmouth's immediate opportunities would be in cranberries[21]. They were native to the area and used by the Wampanoags for food[22], dye, and medicine. They had been grown commercially since 1816 when it was found that they thrived in the swamps and low-lying marshland so common to the Cape. The millponds from abandoned mills were also an outstanding environment for growing cranberries. It was hard work creating cranberry bogs, and harvesting them was even more labor intensive. At first they were hand picked by women and children, but that changed with the invention of the first cranberry scoop in 1887 which favored strength and endurance over the manual dexterity required for picking individual berries. In 1885, Falmouth had 26 acres of cranberries bogs; ten years later, 15,000 barrels of cranberries were shipped from Falmouth. The proliferation of cranberry bogs required cheap labor; wages were kept low so company shareholders could earn 25% to 30% premiums. Portuguese workers, primarily from the Azores and Cape Verde[23] Islands, were a big part of the answer. Dissatisfied workers from the mills, eager to escape the stifling air, low wages, long hours, dangerous machinery, and the lung-destroying dust of the carding rooms, learned of other opportunities for those willing to work hard and were attracted to the area.

---

20   The price of wool declined from 57 cents a pound in 1835 to 25 cents a pound in the 1840's.

21   Growers in 1890: Barzillai C. Cahoon, John C, Crocker, Captain Abishia Phinney, and John T. Sherman.

22   Pemmican cakes were made with cranberries, deer fat, and meal; succotash is made with cranberries, corn, and beans. Sauce was made by boiling them with sugar.

23   Cape Verde became an independent republic in 1975.

Around 1895, the strawberry industry took root. The light sandy soil so unsuitable for most other crops was ideal for strawberries. Most of the land had been abandoned to scrub oak and pitch pines, and was relatively inexpensive. As a result, it provided a good opportunity for people willing and able to leverage their meager resources with sweat equity.

IMMIGRANTS OF IMMIGRANTS

The Portuguese have been emigrating ever since Prince Henry[24] sparked the Age of Discovery. The world's first and longest lived global empire was the Portuguese Empire, beginning with Ceuta in 1415 and formally ending in 1999 with the turnover of Macau to China. It included territories in what are today forty-nine different sovereign states. During the nineteenth century, significant numbers began emigrating to countries that were not part of the Portuguese Empire. Today, there are easily over 100 million people across the globe with Portuguese roots.

Immigration patterns vary dramatically by time period, origin, and destination. The largest Portuguese population is in Brazil. Over 700,000 Portuguese had emigrated to Brazil by 1760, sixteen years before the United States declared its independence from Great Britain.

On Cape Cod, however, most Portuguese immigrants are from the Azores, an area that was itself uninhabited four hundred years earlier.

---

24 Son of King John I of Portugal. Also known as Prince Henry the Navigator, Henrique d'Infante, Duke of Viseu, and Grandmaster of the Order of Christ.

AZOREAN IMMIGRATION

When the islands were discovered in 1432, the Portuguese monarchy ordered them settled for economic, political, and military reasons. Portuguese settlers came from southern Portugal, recently conquered Ceuta, and recently settled Madeira, but many came from other areas[25]. So many immigrants came from Flanders[26] that by 1490 the Azores were often referred to as the Flemish Islands.

CONDITIONS IN THE AZORES AND CAPE VERDE

Portuguese monarchs doled out land in the Azores to the royal family and the aristocracy, setting up a Captain-donatary system so absentee landowners could collect payments from peasant tenants. The Captains-donatary also owned key monopolies like grist mills, collecting 10 percent for the monarchy and one percent for themselves; they were, in effect, commander-in-chief, governors, judges, and Chief Executive Officers, with a tight hand on the land and the people trying to live on it. The nineteenth century book "Description of the Azores, or Western Islands", described it as

"Impolitic, atrocious, replete with all the lamentable causes of despotism...the power and prerogatives enjoyed by the Captain General were considerably greater and less controlled than those even by the King. He possessed supreme

---

25   Including France, Scotland, England, Jews fleeing the Inquisition, Spanish clergy, Moorish prisoners, and enslaved Africans.

26   The Flanders region, ruled by the Duke of Burgundy who had married Prince Henry's sister, was in turmoil because of struggles with the British; people readily sought refuge from the rampant death, destruction, illness, and starvation.

power over all municipal governors and judicial authorities; over every department of finance, agriculture, commerce, and navigation: besides which, being commander in chief of the army, he derived thence an additional weight and influence that negated any resistance to his measures, however despotic."

Initially the Captains-donatory lived on the islands, but after two or three generations they returned to the mainland and sent their agents to run things.

Many southern New England immigrants came from the Cape Verde Islands[27], also uninhabited when discovered by the Portuguese twenty-three years after the Azores. The monarchy began colonizing the town of Ribeira Grande (now Cidade Velha) six years later, but immigration patterns were very different from the Azores. In addition to the original colonists from southern Portugal, many Jews exiled during the Spanish Inquisition in Portugal were sent to Cape Verde. The islands were not suitable for farming and were never prosperous except for the transatlantic slave trade[28], which began declining in 1807 but lasted another half century. In addition to free men from North Africa, many slaves also ended up there.

For Azoreans who were not part of the monarchy or their agents, life was unimaginably harsh. Rents were fixed, regardless of whether crops failed or not. As population increased, starvation was not uncommon. Peasants who owned animals lived with them; the animals inhabited

---

27   Verde in Portuguese means green, a name given to the islands because of the lush vegetation that existed at the time of discovery, a description not appropriate after the droughts and over farming that began in the eighteenth century.

28   Of all the abominable aspects of slavery, in terms of the number of people subjected to sheer brutality, inhumane living conditions, and high mortality rates, the transatlantic slave trade was by far the most offensive.

the first floor of their primitive subsistence homes while the people lived on the second. A peasant's right to work the land typically passed from father to oldest son, who was morally responsible for taking care of his siblings, a situation that became more untenable with each successive generation. There were frequent earthquakes and volcanic activity, but peasants did not have the resources to move elsewhere. They were a deeply religious people[29], almost all of them Catholics, receiving not only spiritual sustenance from their faith but also education for their children from Catholic schools. Families were honored when members became priests, monks, or nuns.

The vast majority of Azoreans were beyond poor, not unlike serfs in a medieval feudal society. Change had not come as quickly to the islands as it had to continental Europe. As bad as things had been, they worsened after Napoleon's invasion of Portugal in 1807. The monarchy fled to Brazil, leaving behind civil administrators who needed young men and a war chest, and who also diminished the Church. The turmoil of the Peninsular War, the War of the Two Brothers, and the Portuguese Civil War, did not end until 1833. The monarchy would ultimately be eliminated in 1910.

---

29   Joseph Sylvester, an 1886 immigrant, said that when he was a boy he could see the stars through the holes in the roof over his sleeping area. He had shoes but was only allowed to wear them in Church; he walked the three miles to Church barefoot, put his shoes on when he reached the church stairs, and when mass was over, returned to the stairs, removed the shoes, returning home barefoot carrying them. Joseph is one of the many strawberry farmers who later contributed to Saint Anthony's church.

AMERICAN IMMIGRATION

Emigration in significant numbers began with the arrival of whaling ships from New England. Initially these ships came from Nantucket and Cape Cod, but after a few decades most came from New Bedford. They came to the Azores to resupply their ships, and to both the Azores and Cape Verde for quiet, hard-working men particularly good at harpooning and ship steering. In the nineteenth century many whalers arrived in the Azores and Cape Verde with skeleton crews because it was cheaper than using Americans who increasingly sought safer work with less personal sacrifice. Whalers also used the Azores as a shipping depot, dropping off whalebones[30] and barrels of whale oil for shipment back home. Both the Azores and Cape Verde provided facilities for ship repair.

Whaling ships from New England began arriving in the Azores as early as 1730, primarily in the Pico-Fayal anchorage. On board the ship, meals were good and there was the promise of a share of the profits at the end of the voyage. When the whaler completed its voyage, the Azoreans, with real money often for the first time, decided to stay in this new world of opportunity to realize the possibility of owning land and reaping its benefits.

Newcomers did not know what living conditions were really like on board a whaler: starvation, violence, high mortality rates, and relatively little money considering the years spent at sea. They did not know that American whalers left with skeleton crews because they could not find enough American seamen, or that it was quicker and easier

---

30   This refers not to the skeleton, but to the baleen found inside the mouths of krill-eating (toothless) whales. It was the plastic or spring steel of its day.

to get them in the Portuguese islands. On the other hand, life was so harsh and unpromising in the Azores that even if they had known, odds are they would have seized the opportunity anyway. Generations of disenfranchisement, frustration, and disillusionment had taken their toll; some islanders became fatalistic, while others with more faith in themselves than in their government became immigrants

In the nineteenth century Azoreans began emigrating to the United States, doing so in three distinct waves:

- Whaling ventures, 1840 to 1870. American whaling peaked in the early to mid 1800s. More whalers came from New Bedford than all other ports combined. These immigrants typically faced whaling voyages of two to four years before reaching America. Many settled in the New Bedford area, and some returned to the Azores even if only between voyages. Their stories about America spread throughout the islands. Many wrote home, often sending money to their families to help out, and encouraging their emigration. Life was hard on family members who stayed behind, and even tougher on many who emigrated on sailing ships: they had to endure voyages of five weeks or longer, many suffering and even perishing from diseases that flourished in primitive overcrowded unregulated living conditions dictated primarily by ship's profits.
- American expansion, 1870 to 1920. Economic growth created a huge demand for workers in textile factories and farms. Metal-hulled steamships cut travel time from the Azores to America from

five weeks to, initially, twelve days and later to nine. Upper passenger decks replaced the auxiliary sails on early steamers, increasing passenger capacity. American financial interests encouraged immigration and actively promoted opportunities in America; some even hired representatives to travel from town to town in the Azores actively encouraging people to emigrate. This ended abruptly when the Immigration Restriction Act of 1921 essentially slammed the door, limiting immigration in each country to 3% per year of the residents from that country, as documented in the 1910 United States Census.

- Volcanic disruption, 1957 to 1980. The historic year-long volcanic eruptions on Faial in 1957-1958 lead to the Azorean Refugee Acts of 1958-1960 and an increase in immigration of over 100,000 people over the next ten years. Most went to work in factories, but many others started small businesses. These Acts were spearheaded by then Senator John F. Kennedy, and his portrait is still found in many Portuguese homes.

SETTLING IN FALMOUTH

Many Portuguese immigrants from the Azores and Cape Verdean islands originally came to Falmouth after first settling somewhere else. Frequently they came from New Bedford or the Taunton area, but also from other towns as far west as Narragansett Bay. They found work in the cranberry bogs, on farms, and as laborers.

Manuel Viera Martins, known as "Tio Calhau" (pronounced "Tee-cal-YOW"), the first Portuguese person to acquire land in Waquoit, was among the first of the three waves of immigrants. He was born on Pico in 1855. His ancestors had fled England to avoid the persecution of Roman Catholics that began with Henry VIII.

Tio Calhau shipped out in 1867 on the New Bedford whaling bark Kathleen, completing the voyage four years later in New Bedford, where he collected his 1/140th share of the profits. In 1875, he signed on for another whaling trip on the Kathleen and shortly after it anchored between the islands of Faial and Pico for recruitment and replenishment, he jumped ship and swam ashore to return home[31]. In this, he was fortunate; the Kathleen was later stove and sunk [32] by a whale.

Tio Calhau married Maria Josefa Rodrigues from Candelaria, Pico, in 1878 and they emigrated to America in 1883, settling in New Bedford. He went on one more whaling voyage but when he attempted to go on another, his wife gave him an ultimatum: stay home or stay at sea for good. Tio Calhau never went whaling again.

In 1893, he purchased the Riverside Cottage in Waquoit. He and his eleven-year-old son, John, worked long hard backbreaking hours clearing the land to plant strawberries, a relatively new cash crop for Falmouth. They planted runners in August, covered the plants with pine needles, and picked their first crop the next spring. During the offseason, he sold firewood and worked as a laborer.

---

31   There are so many stories of Azoreans on whaleboats jumping ship when they arrived in a desired port that some of them joked about using whaleboats like a bus.

32   Rammed and rendered unseaworthy, sometimes by a whale striking it at full speed from underneath but more often from the surface. In either case, the result was the same: the hull was compromised and the ship sank.

Tio Calhau was not the first Portuguese landowner in the area; that distinction belonged to Francisco da Rosa Perry, another whaling man from Pico. Francisco, a/k/a Frank Perry, had previously lived in East Providence, RI, with his first wife Mary Ann (also from Pico), raising six children until her death in 1889. He married the widow Antonia George Souza, a neighbor-friend in East Providence who already had four children, and who was also from Pico. In 1889 they moved to Falmouth, buying the Nathaniel Swift house on Fresh Pond (345 Carriage Shop Road).

The United States Census of 1900 lists 142 Falmouth residents with Portuguese heritage. It was a relatively young population: 87 had been born in the United States. Of the 55 Portuguese immigrants, all but one were from the Azores, including all 20 of the male heads of household.

Fifty-five immigrants, 20 of them heads of households, with an unusually cohesive faith, traditions, and language, but also with almost no resources except their sweat and each other, in an established town of 3,000. Their geographically insular homeland became a socially insular new world. And together they thrived.

One of the key traditions that fostered their unity was the Festa do Divino Espírito Santo, celebrated in every island of the Azores at Impérios, small buildings built specifically for that purpose. Frank Perry, who had acquired land in Falmouth from his whaler earnings, gifted a parcel on Carriage Shop Road in 1900 for the use of the Holy Ghost Society[33] of which he was a devoted member. Tio Calhau, known for his sing-song banter, would become its first auctioneer. Manuel G. Dutra from Hatchville, the third Portuguese landowner, would also become a founding

---

33   He also hoped that eventually a church would be built there.

member, as would early landowners Francisco Teixeira, John Souza, Manuel Cunha, Antone Souza, Joe Silvia White, and Joseph Sylvester.

HISTORY OF THE FEAST OF THE HOLY SPIRIT.

The Feast of the Holy Spirit is a long tradition in Portugal, dating back to a Franciscan convent in 1296[34] Alenquer (near Lisbon) established by Queen Isabella of Portugal. It is no longer widely commemorated on mainland Portugal[35], but in the volcanic islands of the Azores it is perhaps the most important holy day of the year.

Princess Isabella (medieval Portuguese spelling Helizabeth) of Aragon was the eldest daughter of King Pedro III of Aragon and Constance of Sicily. She was a descendant of Holy

---

34   Montez says Queen Elizabeth may have introduced it as early as 1296 in Alenquer, north of Lisbon.

35   It was suppressed on the mainland by the First Republic, which deposed the monarchy in 1810, but was less successful in the more independent Azores, thanks in part to its geographic separation by 850 miles of ocean.

Roman Emperor Frederic II and the niece of Saint Elizabeth of Hungary. Isabella was raised as a devout princess, attending Mass daily, a practice she continued throughout her life. At the age of twelve, while being sought in marriage by the Kings of England and Spain for their sons, she was married by proxy to King Dinis of Portugal, sixth king on the throne and the first to rule

Sta Isabel Reyna de Portugal Patrona de la V.O.T. de Penitencia de

a Portugal free from the Moors. Dinis did not actually meet his child bride until 18 months later.

Dinis was a good king but by today's standards was not initially a good husband. After a brief war between Portugal and Castile, he generally avoided war and did much to gain recognition of Portugal as an independent country, no small task when much of Europe was in seemingly perpetual conflict. Dinis ended a diplomatic conflict with the Catholic Church, granted asylum to Templar knights that were being persecuted in France, and established the Order of Christ as a continuation of the Order of the Temple (Knights Templar). Dinis is sometimes called the Farmer King; he developed rural areas, redistributed land, built castles, created new towns, promoted agriculture, ordered exploration of iron, tin, copper, and silver mines, established markets, and increased exports including signing the first commercial agreement with England in 1308. After his marriage to Isabella, he founded several social institutions and improved the legal code to protect the lower classes from abuse and extortion; it must be assumed she was not without influence in this.

Queen Isabella was a devout person, "full of the Holy Spirit." She spent much of her life in prayer and helping the sick and poor, as witnessed by many legends still recited to this day. She interceded to avert warfare between her son, the future King Afonso IV, and Dinis' illegitimate son Afonso Sanches. Isabella founded institutions for the sick, for travelers, for wayward women, and for abandoned infants. She established a convent for nuns and provided dowries for poor brides. She helped raise and tutor most of Dinis' illegitimate children. When her husband King Dinis died, like her Aunt Saint Elizabeth of Hungary, she relinquished court dress for the habit of the Third Franciscan Order, living the remainder of her days adjacent to the "Poor Clares" convent she established. She did not renounce the crown, instead using her royal resources to continue helping the sick and poor. In advanced age and illness she rode for many days on a mule to Estremoz, where her son King Afonso IV and the King of Castile were preparing for battle. Her intercession again averted war, but she died in Estremoz shortly afterward.

The most popular and persistent legend about her is the miracle of the roses. Queen Isabella, much to the displeasure of her husband, would bring food from her kitchen to feed the poor, carrying it in the fold of her garments. On one such occasion at the castle of Sambucus, she was seen leaving the garden by the King, who asked what she was carrying. She replied "roses, my lord." He asked to see them, and when she unfolded her garments, roses appeared instead of the food she had been carrying.[36]

Another legend is that Queen Isabella, troubled by plight of the starving poor, pleaded with the Holy Ghost, even offering to sell her jewels including her crown. Soon two ships appeared in a harbor, unmanned, with cattle and grain. It was thought to be a miracle from the Holy Ghost, and a feast was given for the poor.

Her concern for the sick is related in another legend where, after she had helped lepers, one of them was beaten by a royal guard. This person was later brought to Elizabeth, who washed the wounds with egg whites to help stop the bleeding.

Whatever their source, these legends attest to the popular sentiment for a Queen who deeply cared for the unfortunate and disadvantaged.

After her death on July 11, 1335, in accordance with her will, her body was transported from Estremoz to the Monastery of Santa Clara-a-Velha. Well into the trip, liquid began seeping from holes that developed in the coffin. However, the odor was not the stench of a decomposing corpse; rather, it was said to be a pleasant sweet smell.

Isabella of Aragon, Queen of Portugal, was beatified by Pope Leo X in 1516 and was canonized by Pope Urban VIII in 1624. She is revered on July 4, the "official" date of her death.

In time, the convent of Santa Clara-a-Velha in Coimbra, where Queen Isabella was first laid to rest in a Gothic sarcophagus, was overtaken by the river Mondego. In the seventeenth century, the new convent of Santa Clara-a-Nova was built and Queen Isabella's body was placed in a

---

36   Some attribute this legend to her Aunt, Queen Elizabeth of Hungary.

new tomb of silver and crystal. The room in which Queen Isabella died was later made into a chapel. Today, she is the patron saint of Coimbra and a patron saint of brides, of charities, and of victims of adultery; many schools and churches bear her name.

Although royalty began this tradition, over time commoners adopted it and silver crowns and scepters were used instead of the original royal gold crown inset with precious jewels. The tradition was probably brought to the Azores by the Franciscans, who were amongst the early settlers. The crown and scepter used in most festas today have a dove atop the crown, and also at the tip of the scepter, to honor Queen Isabella as an instrument of the Holy Spirit.

Holy Ghost Society of Fresh Pond

People say Saint Anthony's church in East Falmouth was built with strawberries. When it was constructed in 1924, Portuguese strawberry farmers, many of whom had for years donated one day's strawberry sales to the church, funded most of it. Today, there is a stained glass window in Saint Anthony's church depicting strawberry farmers to commemorate this heritage. Many of these farmers came from the Fresh Pond area.

But long before there was a church in East Falmouth, there were Holy Ghost halls. The first was built in Fresh Pond, near Waquoit, in 1900 by the Waquoit Holy Ghost Association. In 1911, another group formed in East Falmouth and built St. Anthony's Hall on Brick Kiln Road. In both halls, prayers were led by elders on Sundays and holy days of obligation. In 1921, a traveling priest[37] was assigned to say Mass at the altars in the halls.

But before that, before there was even a hall in Fresh Pond, there was sopas — a meal that included beef, broth, and mint — the centerpiece of an annual tradition celebrated on all Azores islands.

In the 1880's the newly arrived immigrants celebrated it in their homes, joining together with other immigrants.

As their numbers increased, they could not be contained in a single home. Much like the early days of Azorean settlement, when sopas was brought to homes on Pentecost Sunday in ox and goat wagons, the founding members of the Holy Ghost Society cooked huge pots of sopas and delivered it to homes in horse drawn wagons. People awaiting the wagon would greet them with prayers, cheers, and empty panellas. In homes where people were too sick to go to the wagon, the members ran to the door to get the panellas, filled them at the wagon, and returned them to the house. One way or another, the wagon left a trail of full panellas and smiling faces in its wake.

In ascending order of immigration, here is a list of the founding families using their Americanized names. Where spouses are known to have immigrated in different years, the wife's immigration year is shown in parentheses.

1875   Manuel and Mary (????) Dutra
1880   Francisco and Mary Ann Perry da Rosa

---

37   Reverend Antonio M. Fortuna, assistant pastor of Santo Cristo in Fall River, Massachusetts was given this assignment by Bishop Daniel J. Feehan of the Diocese of Fall River, after an appeal to him from the Portuguese community in East Falmouth. He would become the first pastor of Saint Anthony's church.

1883	Manuel and Maria Josefa Martin.
1887	Joseph and Evarista (1878) Sylvester
1889	Joseph and Philomena Andrews
1892	Antone and Mary (1889) Souza
1895	Joseph and Maria Rosa White
1897	Anthony Brown
1900	Francisco and Maria Teixeira
1901	Manuel and Mary Cunha
1902	John and Mary (1909) Souza
n/a	Manuel G. and Martina (b1910) Souza

In 1900, there were only twenty male heads of households from the Azores in Falmouth. That means almost half of them[38] banded together to form the Fresh Pond Holy Ghost Association.[39]

While the land for the annual festa was donated, the members wanted a building, like the Impérios in the Azores, with an altar to hold the crown and a place to store everything needed to prepare for and host the celebration. The Império was the focal point of the festa. As frugal and debt averse as they would be with their own homes, the members wanted to pay cash for whatever they did and were willing to work hard building it themselves to keep costs down.

They found an abandoned boat paint shop in Waquoit, bought the building outright, and agreed to remove it and restore it on Perry's donated land. They designed a hall

38   Two of the twelve were not Falmouth residents when the society was founded. Joseph Sylvester was then a resident of Taunton, and Manuel Cunha was a resident of Barnstable. Anthony Brown, a founder, was not a head of household.

39   The United States census records for 1890 were destroyed, and the portions that were salvageable were discarded, so it is impossible to ascertain the Portuguese population in Falmouth at that time.

similar to many in the Azores: a one room building with a center double door and windows on both sides, with an alcove in the rear part of the building for an altar to house the Holy Ghost, one that could be built almost entirely with just the materials from the boat paint shop.

The members dug the foundation with a horse drawn scoop, straightening the sides with hand shovels. Some lumber from the paint shop was used to make forms for the foundation walls, which were poured in several courses using hand mixed cement; when one course was dried, they removed the forms, raised them up a level, and poured the next one. When the foundation was complete, the wood from the forms was used in the hall itself; nothing was wasted. The hall originally had an altar for storing and displaying the crown, and additional space inside for meetings and small gatherings. Cooking was done outside the hall on a wood burning stove, while eating was done outside on makeshift tables. Bathroom facilities consisted of an outhouse on the rear perimeter of the cleared land.

An annual festa has been held every year on this site since its donation. With few exceptions, it has always been held on Pentecost Sunday, the end of the Easter season in the Catholic Church, celebrating the descent of the Holy Spirit on the Apostles.

There were no Roman Catholic churches nearby; the nearest was in Woods Hole. The elders began using their altar for religious purposes, including saying rosaries. Eventually a traveling priest began saying masses there, not unlike the judges who used to ride circuits from town to town.

Francisco Perry had hoped that someday a church might be built on the property, but in 1924 Saint Anthony's church was built in East Falmouth, about two miles from Fresh

Pond. Most Portuguese travelled there either on foot or in a horse drawn wagon. Many owned or worked on strawberry farms. In those days, most farmers grew a variety of strawberry called Howard 17's and the season was only six weeks long. Berries had to be picked daily. And so, during strawberry season, an early mass was said very early at the hall so they could still have a full day to pick strawberries.

The Holy Ghost hall changed little until the 1930s. A tent was purchased to shelter the people eating outside. The hall itself was well maintained but not modified until 1935, when members bought lumber and bricks to extend the hall, add a new furnace, and reshingle the exterior. In 1936, the west side of the property was fenced in using posts donated by Antone Souza and wire donated by Charles Sylvia. Other major repairs were made, overseen by Manuel S. White Sr., Frank Souza, and Jack Lopes. In 1938, the original stone arch - the one my brother and I climbed in the early nineteen fifties - was built.

World War II, with its need for material resources and young men, meant that the property remained unchanged until the middle of the decade. The eight-year period after the war ended saw the greatest property changes in the history of the society:

- 1946: a new commercial stove was purchased for $169[40].
- 1948: members donated a new water heater (Fred Rose), boiler (Joe Ferreira), and pump (Antone Souza). The membership began discussions about toilet facilities. The building committee (Manuel White, Jesse Torres, Joe Teixeira, Frank M Teixeira,

---

40   Journal, p.94

Alfred Soares) recommended bringing the beer stand closer to the hall and expanding it for $375, more than half of which was for plumbing.

- 1950: Newly elected building committee chairman Joe Teixeira spearheaded rebuilding the kitchen and ice cream stand, erecting a new flag pole, and installing a public address system with a record player. In September of the following year, a membership work party extended the hall, increasing the kitchen to 45'x22'. Lot boundaries were also changed; members accepted Joe Ferreira's offer to exchange 70' of frontage in front for 70' in back. Two years after that, Joe Teixeira and Manuel S. White, Sr added a large indoor dining room at the rear of the hall. Until 1952, sopas had been eaten in a huge tent erected solely for that purpose.

For the next thirty years, the hall and grounds remained largely unchanged. In 1985, food concessions were moved from the right side of the building to the left side to make room for indoor bathrooms and an office on the right side. The bandstand was moved from the front of the building to the rear west side where it sits today.

In the last 25 years, except for maintenance, the building has remained unchanged as the society focused more on the grounds, adding a large asphalt driveway, landscaping, and tables, picnic tables, benches, and umbrellas for socializing and enjoying the auction and music after the sopas have been served. The arch was damaged in a motor vehicle accident in 2008 but was rebuilt the following year with an improvement: the new arch included sockets for medium sized flagpoles.

THE FESTA

Two crowns and scepters were brought to this country by Tio Carassa (Jose Silveira de Andrade, aka Joe Andrews) when he immigrated from Fayal in 1889. He owned one set, and the other was owned by his father, Jose Marcelinho de Andrade; the fact that Tio Carassa brought them both clearly indicates his intention to continue the Holy Ghost tradition in the new country. He gave one set to the Fresh Pond group and the other to the Santuit group.

The festa begins when a procession brings the crown to the hall and places it on the altar. Originally it began at a member's home and proceeded directly to the hall. In later years, after Saint Anthony's was built, a small procession went first to the church, where the designated queen was crowned, followed by the procession, which began at Fonseca Park, about a half mile from the hall.

The small procession grew over the years. By the 1950s, it was led by members of the society, the queen and her court, a band, members of the Sisters[41] of the Holy Ghost praying an oversized rosary during the procession, and decorated vehicles. Members of the queen's court wore special headpieces called the "tongues of fire,"[42] reminiscent of the vision of the Holy Spirit appearing on Earth. The

---

41 The original Fresh Pond Holy Ghost Society was referred to as a brotherhood because it consisted entirely of men. Women, of course, were active in preparing for the festa, but in a supporting role. In 1952 Elsie Teixeira founded a women's counterpart referred to as the Sisters of the Holy Ghost, which expanded the role and contributions made by women.

42 And when the day of Pentecost was fully come, they were all with one accord in one place. 2And suddenly there came a sound from heaven as of a rushing mighty wind, and it filled all the house where they were sitting. 3And there appeared unto them cloven tongues like as of fire, and it sat upon each of them. 4And they were all filled with the Holy Ghost, and began to speak with other tongues, as the Spirit gave them utterance. King James Bible, Act 2, verses 1:4

procession ended in front of the hall and, with the queen and her court standing on the steps facing the crowd, the band played the traditional Hino do Espirito Santo (Hymn of the Holy Spirit). The queen and her court then proceeded with dignity to the altar where the crown was placed on a special display.

Traditionally, the band played for their meal, so they were the first to eat the sopas. When they were done, the band regrouped on the bandstand and played traditional Portuguese music while the members (the workers) ate next. After that, doors were opened to the general public and all who went to the door were welcomed for the free meal and ate until they were satisfied.

Inside the main hall, the Sisters hosted a raffle and, in later years, a Chinese auction. Many people socialized and browsed items that would later be auctioned.

Concession stands on the side of the building sold food and refreshments from the time the band finished playing the Hymn of the Holy Spirit until closing. There were ice cream, peanuts, candy, and a variety of Portuguese dishes including tremoços[43], favas, cacoila, linguiça, and bifana. Refreshments featured home made Portuguese wine, soft drinks, and water. As appropriate for an organization founded by hard working people with few resources, all were priced significantly lower than generally available elsewhere; the goal was only to cover expenses and have enough left over to conduct the next festa.

Shortly after the meal was over, an auction was held to raise money to cover all club expenses, including the cost of the sopas. Auction items were donated by the members. In

---

43   Lupini beans soaked in salted water, usually eaten by squeezing the skin and popping the bean into your mouth.

the old days, these sometimes represented a promise made to the Holy Spirit for the granting of a request, but more often than not they were simply acts of generosity. Most of the people bidding for auction items did so in the generous spirit of Queen Elizabeth. I still remember, back in the 1960s when I had my first real job, bidding $12 for a loaf of massa sovada (Portuguese sweet bread). The outrageous betting was marked by much laughter and bravado, fed by a sometimes humorous but always effective auctioneer.

The Sisters of the Holy Ghost also hosted a raffle and creative activities like face painting and a variety of games for children.

MEMBERS

Membership is by invitation only. Members must be of Portuguese heritage, or the parent of a child with Portuguese heritage. The husband of a Portuguese woman is eligible on the assumption they will have children.

Religion is very important. Members must be practicing Catholics in good standing with the Church. Prayers are recited during the Domingas, and an annual Mass is held for the society. In 1951, memberships voted to formalize the practice of having all members present the night before the funeral of a member to recite the rosary.

Members are expected to actively participate in society activities, including work parties and preparation and conduct of the feast. The major expansion after World War II was marked by many votes illustrating this: one example required "all members to report for work on the addition Sunday, September 30, 1951 at 9 a.m."

In addition to the time and effort members contribute to support the society, they also provide direct financial support through dues, but this is largely a matter of conscience. Prior to World War II, strawberry farmers donated one case of strawberries each year to the society, but this was encouraged only and not enforced. Since 1949, long-standing members who pass their sixty-fifth birthday are typically voted honorary members for life without dues, but many who qualify for this continue paying dues regardless.

It has always been a patriotic organization, suspending dues for members who joined the military.

And the members supported each other; when one member lost everything in a fire, brothers individually helped furnish his new home with appliances, furniture, linens, dishes, and cookware.

THE SMALL CROWN

The origins of the Small Crown are unknown. Fresh Pond HGS records refer to it as early as 1935, but there is no mention of it again until 1949 when records show the organization accepted the Small Crown from another group. There is little information on this group other than a statement in the Brotherhood journals that Small Crown members who were not Catholic must convert if they wished to join the group.

The Small Crown festa was first held in 1949 and has been held a few weeks after Pentecost every year since. The Sisters of the Holy Ghost formalized their organization in 1952, with Elsie Teixeira as President. They have their own domingas, featuring the Small Crown as its focus. At one time the Small Crown festa was known as the "little feast" and also as the "children's feast," and was run by the Sisters. Over the years, this distinction has been lost and the little feast is now run by the Brothers.

ADDITIONAL USES OF THE HALL

It was natural that the Brothers would find common cause in supporting each other. The hall was used for social occasions and entertainment (dances, traditional card games of bisca, sueca, and whist, volleyball, shooting pool), and also for meetings of groups like strawberry growers and the Falmouth Shellfish Association. During the 1930s the Portuguese-American Civic League used the hall without charge[44]. The association also allowed other groups to use the hall for a small fee (like the Cab Drivers of Falmouth), but its use for profitable commercial use is expressly forbidden.

Since the beginning, the hall has been used for members' special occasions, including baptisms and wedding receptions. It seems logical that it would have been used for weddings before Saint Anthony's Church was built, but there is no documented proof that it was.

Proper decorum has always been important. For example, in 1949 the society voted that, "no one to play cards or shoot pool while there are dances going on". In 1950, the group bought a ping-pong table and volleyball set but stipulated these could not be used immediately prior to the festa.

In 1951, a committee formed by the HGS (John F. Ferreira, chair; Jesse Costa, Anthony Souza) met with the

---

44   The HGS also allowed them to borrow items on an ad hoc basis, such as flags for a parade.

Board of Trade to discuss the forthcoming Strawberry Festival. They also loaned the tent to St. Anthony's club for a clambake.

Today the society sponsors breakfasts, from 7a.m.to 11 a.m., the first Sunday of each month in the spring, summer, and fall. In addition to the annual Festa do Divino Espirito Santo, it also sponsors a "small Feast[45]" later in the summer and a pig roast in early fall.

All association monies are used for the festa, donations to charitable causes, and maintaining the hall itself.

OTHER LOCAL PORTUGUESE ORGANIZATIONS

EAST FALMOUTH HOLY GHOST ASSOCIATION

The East Falmouth Holy Ghost Association was founded by another group of Portuguese immigrants but it was a separate and distinct organization. Unlike the Fresh Pond Holy Ghost Society, the East Falmouth Association was part of the IDES, whereas the Fresh Pond HGS was independent of it. Like Fresh Pond, the East Falmouth building also became a local social center. Eventually, there was disagreement between the pastor of Saint Anthony's and the East Falmouth Holy Ghost Association over control of the festivities and what it viewed as the semi-religious functions performed by the IDES. The Holy Ghost Association of East Falmouth stopped having a feast

---

45   See the "Small Crown" section of this book for more information.

as a result of this friction, and in the early 1930s deeded their hall to Saint Anthony's Club, while continuing its social functions. Since then, the Feast of the Holy Ghost in Falmouth has been celebrated only in the Fresh Pond hall.

PORTUGUESE-AMERICAN CIVIC LEAGUE (PACL)

The Portuguese-American Civic League (PACL) of Massachusetts was established in 1930 to promote the civic, political, educational, and social welfare of Portuguese families. The Falmouth council was organized in 1933. The Holy Ghost Society of Fresh Pond was an active supporter. In 1935, the Falmouth PACL used the hall without charge to teach boys and girls a few amusements for the benefit of the PACL.[46] The Holy Ghost Society also agreed to let PACL borrow flags, and in 1936 helped the PACL with relief for the flood.

One of the most important activities of the PACL was its assistance with the citizenship naturalization process.

Mrs. Joseph J. Costa (maiden name Mary Mello Cardeiro) and Mrs. Joaquim M. Sambade were among the most active members.

The Falmouth PACL is no longer active.

---

46   Portuguese-American Civic League of Plymouth.   There is a contract for a band dated April 20, 1938 showing "Plymouth Post, No. 40, American Legion Band" on the letter; there are about 40 members in the band photo.   Joseph S. Contente, manager, signed the contract.

PORTUGUESE-AMERICAN ASSOCIATION (PAA) (THE NAVEGADOR)

The PAA was founded in 1979 to:

1. Initiate, sponsor, encourage, and promote Portuguese cultural activities within the upper Cape Cod area of Massachusetts;

2. Instill among members of the Portuguese-American community a sense of pride in their heritage;

3. Encourage the study of Portuguese history, language, art and sciences;

4. Promote among the members of the Portuguese-American Association a genuine feeling of warmth and good fellowship.

Today there are almost 200 members in the PAA. Membership is open to any person of good moral character who manifests a genuine interest in the mission of the organization.

It is easily the largest and most active Portuguese organization in Falmouth. It respects the dates of the Fresh Pond Holy Ghost Society and IDES festas, hosting instead the Day of Portugal on the nearest weekend to the official Portuguese holiday of June 10; this almost always places it between the two festas. Other annual events typically include an Easter egg hunt, Portuguese Dinner Dance in April, a clam boil in late August, and a harvest dinner dance in late October. In spring, summer, and fall, it hosts breakfasts on the second Sunday of every month, from 7 am - 11:30 a.m. In the charitable spirit of the Holy Ghost, every year the PAA provides facilities, coordination, and labor for a community effort to provide free Thanksgiving dinners to anyone who shows up; it even helps deliver them to people who are housebound; in 2010 the organization served over 1,000 dinners.

Navegador facilities, including a function room seating 180 with a wooden dance floor, a full kitchen, a full size patio, and an outdoor barbecue, are available for rent by the general public. It is a very civic-minded organization, providing reduced rental rates (essentially at cost) for non-profit and youth organizations insofar as they are not inconsistent with the Portuguese American Association mission statement.

Prelude to the Festa

The festa today remains the focal point of an annual cycle that the founders began on Trinity Sunday (one week after Pentecost) when members met to draw lots for the honor of having the crown in their homes for one of the seven weeks between Easter and Pentecost Sunday. In recent years the Fresh Pond HGS has drawn lots the evening of the festa to determine who hosts the crown in each of the seven weeks next year..

There are, of course, many practical matters that need to be handled. Finances must be sufficient to cover not only the festa itself, but also maintenance, operating expenses, and taxes for the facilities. Fund-raising events are sometimes necessary to fill expense gaps. Breakfasts are hosted the first Sunday of every month, except during the winter, for this purpose.

Like so many other things in today's society, the festa preparations have become more complicated. In the early days, a cow or bull was purchased or sometimes donated for the feast. The animal was slaughtered and dressed outside, then carried to the basement for butchering. In those days of a more active farming community, before meat was purchased in plastic packaging, children would gather to observe the matança[47]. In the early days, as in the old country, the bladder was used as a kick ball by the children playing outside while their older relatives were preparing for the festa. The meat was carried downstairs where it hung for a couple of days before it was butchered, and the remains were buried out back. A priest blessed meat for the traditional sopas at least 24 hours before it was served to allow sufficient time for cooking.

Nowadays things are not as simple. Health concerns make it impractical to slaughter and butcher an animal at the hall, so packaged USDA approved meat is purchased. The kitchen must be inspected and licensed before food can be prepared. Licenses must also be procured for liquor and even for the event itself. Sometimes members have to forego hosting the crown because of insurance concerns[48]. A procession is legally a parade, which also now requires a permit.

DOMINGAS

A dominga is any one of the seven weeks between Easter and Pentecost when the crown is at a member's home to celebrate the Holy Spirit. Hosts decorate their homes with flowers, prepare a special altar area to hold the crown, and are always ready for guests. For each of the seven Saturdays between Easter Sunday and Pentecost Sunday, members of the Brothers and Sisters of the Holy Ghost gather at a

---

47   Slaughter and butchering of the animal.

48   We may think this is new, but in 1946 Jack Lopes had to relinquish his Dominga to Manny Rapoza because of pressure from his Fire Insurance provider.

dominga home for prayers, refreshment, and socializing. The following day, the crown is moved to the home hosting the next dominga.

The seventh dominga is special. The member hosting the seventh dominga has the honor of choosing a young girl, usually a pre-teen or young teenager, to represent Queen Isabella[49]. On the seventh dominga, the crown is brought to the church for the coronation mass preceding the festa.

In order for a member to qualify for a dominga, he must have attended all seven of the previous years' domingas.

In addition, the Sisters host their own set of domingas with the small crown for their membership. In addition to honoring and celebrating the Holy Ghost, they also prepare for the festa. One of their festa activities is a game of chance for children, where children pick reffers (small piece of twisted paper) from a basket and win a prize if it has a number written inside. During each week of the domingas, the Sisters collect prizes and distribute pieces of paper for each member to twist.

PREPARING THE HALL

The establishment of monthly breakfasts in the spring has made preparation of the hall easier because the building and grounds are generally ready for use. Two weeks before the festa, the Brothers obtain all the liquor and food permits and order 300 lbs. of beef, 200 lbs. of pork, 60 dozen rolls, 100 double loafs of Portuguese bread, 100 lbs.

---

49   Some say the child represents not the Queen herself, but rather commemorates the Queen's charitable act of placing her crown briefly on child as one of her many acts of kindness.

of onions, and four cases of cabbage for sopas. They also order beverages and other foods for the concession stand.

The following week is a beehive of final cleanup inside and outside: the grounds, the hall, the kitchen, the dining room, and the concession area. The altar is decorated to receive the crowns and the auction gifts.

The Friday before the feast, all food is delivered to the hall and placed in storage.

On Saturday, the outside area is set up with picnic tables, an open tent, and bar tables. The bandstand is cleaned and decorated. Flag pennants are strung.

Inside the hall, the Chinese auction tables and raffle area are prepared. All day long, members arrive with gifts for the outside auction and display them on the right side of the altar.

The Sisters are in charge of the children's games, including face painting, the raffle, and the Chinese auction. They collect items during the year and bring them to the hall for setup on Saturday.

Members of the IDES clean and setup a malassadas booth, which they host for the benefit of the Fresh Pond HGS festa.

PREPARING THE MEAL

In the old days, preparation for the main meal began with the arrival of a cow or bull on the Thursday preceding the festa. Today, the week before is spent cleaning the kitchen and scouring the pots, pans, and utensils used to prepare and serve the food. The 80 and 100-quart pots used to cook the food, and the 150-quart separator used to hold the broth, are all steamed for a minimum of 20 minutes before use.

Today, the food is generally brought to the hall early Saturday morning, the day before the festa. The bread is classic Portuguese white bread, a relatively coarse airy bread made with wa-

ter, flour, sugar, and butter. The Sisters slice it the day before and lay the slices on trays to air dry before they are used for sopas. The Sisters also peel the onions and remove any loose leaves from the cabbage. They usually set the tables before helping with food for the concessions, or preparing for other festa activities they are sponsoring.

The priest arrives early Saturday morning to bless the food (see Prayers of Blessing in the Appendix).

COOKING SOPAS

Through experience, members have acquired and constructed tools and techniques for preparing sopas in large quantities. The food is cooked in large (80-100 qt.)

stockpots using long handled spoons, skimmers, two quart scoops, and baskets. A unique homegrown separator eliminates most of the fat from the broth before it is served; basically, it's a huge stockpot with a dispensing nozzle at the bottom where it draws lower fat broth and a strainer at the top to filter pieces of meat and vegetables when broth is transferred from the stockpots. The tools used for stirring, removing the broth, and removing vegetables and meat are also homemade, usually from large long handled pans, wooden extensions, and clamps.

After the beef is blessed, it is cut into strips roughly one hand width wide, trimmed of most fat and gristle, and put in large pots on the floor beside the cutting boards, taking care to stack the meat crosswise so as to leave large gaps around the meat to improve water circulation. In 2010, we used about 300 pounds of meat total, 75 pounds to a pot. The pots have a thick metal screen placed on the bottom before the meat is added to prevent the meat from sticking. Before the pots are placed on the stove, about four inches of water is added.

Sopas is cooked on a large cast iron stove with four main range grates. Under each grate are three concentric burners, each with its own control knob. When all the meat is in the pots, all burners are lit, starting with the innermost ring first.

The meat-filled pots are then lifted to the stove, with the largest pot closest to the separator. They are then filled two-thirds of the way to the top with water. Three spice bags[50] are placed in the largest pot and two in each of the others. Large peeled onions are added: three in the largest

---

50   One of the sisters makes nine snowball size cheesecloth "spice bags" containing mostly pickling spice.

pot and two in each of the others, followed by three cabbage halves in the largest pot, and two in each of the others. All pots are then filled to approximately two inches of the top with water and left to boil, typically taking about two hours. Pieces of meat float to the surface just prior to the water reaching the boiling point. When a boil is reached, each pot is stirred and salt is added at the rate of one large heaped cooking spoon per 20 quarts. The heat is then turned down to a simmer by shutting off 10 of the 12 burners, leaving only the outermost burner on the first and third grate turned on[51]. The meat typically simmers for at least six hours, until it begins to fall apart from its own weight when lifted; sometimes it is left simmering all night.

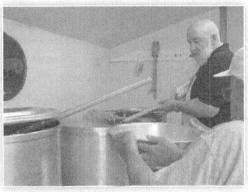

The second day begins at least three hours before serving time. The head cook samples each pot and decides whether more salt is needed; usually the large pot needs a couple more spoonfuls and the smaller pots one each. Sopas broth is uniquely flavored with fresh hortelã, a sweet Portuguese mint, harvested the day before — and sometimes the morning of — the festa. It is heavily interleaved with layers of bread in a panellas before the broth is

---

51   Many years ago, one of the cooks turned a burner down so low that it extinguished the flame, then turned it back up a notch thinking it would be low heat. The gas slowly accumulated until there was a small explosion that was alarming but fortunately harmless. Since then, the practice is to turn each burner either completely off or completely on.

poured over it. Freshly picked hortelã brought by the members is cleaned and the panellas are filled with alternating layers of dried bread and fresh mint, so they are ready to go at serving time.

When the meat is almost done simmering, the separator is set up. A screen is placed in the bottom, and the strainer is placed at the top, suspended above the broth on a copper tube inserted between the strainer handles.

When the meat is cooked, the onions, cabbage, and spice bags are removed and discarded, and the separator burner is lit. Using a custom long handled ladle made from a small pot clamped to a long wooden handle, broth is ladled from each of the pots into the separator until it is half full.

Using another custom made "slotted spoon" (a heavy duty frying basket clamped to another long pole), meat is then moved from each of the three smaller pots to the larger one to make room for vegetables until the largest pot is full.

About an hour and a quarter from serving time, one of the 80 qt. pots is filled with onions, one with cabbage, and the third with a combination of both. If necessary, water is added to fill the pots within two inches of the top. Onions are done 60 minutes after the water begins to boil; the cabbages take

about 30 minutes.

At serving time, all vegetables are removed and with enough meat to get started, all are set on the main table to be cut up for serving. The first bread and mint filled panella is brought to the broth separator where it is filled with enough broth to cover the contents, then it too is brought to the serving table and the food service begins.

A second batch of vegetables is placed into the pots, which is usually sufficient for remaining meals to be served. While food is being served, meat is removed and more bread and mint panellas filled as required, and broth is removed from the pots to keep the separator at least half full at all times. Broth is taken from the rightmost pot; when a pot is empty, it is removed from the stove and cleaned. After food service is completed, some people come to the kitchen door with small pots to get sopas to bring home for those who are sick and unable to come to the festa.

There is always some food left over. Members meet at the hall the next day for a final meal of the sopas. Whatever is still left is brought home by members.

Fresh Pond Festas
2009 - 2011

The 2011 festa began with the queen and her court
bringing the crowns and scepters to the Hall. They
were brought inside and put on display on the left side of
the altar. On the right side of the altar (unseen in this
photograph) are gifts to be auctioned later in the day.

Sopas was served after the crowns were put on display. Members working the festa ate first, usually 11:30 a.m., so the serving line was open by noon. Generally, people were served on a first-come, first-served basis, but senior citizens and the disabled were welcomed at the head of the line at all times. The dining room was set up for 10 tables of eight chairs each. Meals were served family style, with members bringing food from the kitchen as needed. As people left and tables were cleared, more people were welcomed into the dining area to fill them.

The concessions stands on the left side of the hall open early, serving Portuguese dishes like kale soup, jag, shrimp Mozambique, favas, feijoada, Portuguese rice, bacalhau, carne guisada and bifanas, as well as good old American hot dogs with chips, peppers, and onions. Refreshments of soda, beer, and wine are available. Ice cream is served all day long.

While sopas are being served, people socialize. There are games of chance for children as well as things like face-painting; others seek out malassadas (fried dough) as soon as they smell it. Many adults prefer the quieter areas inside the hall where they can socialize while looking over items offered in the Chinese auction or buying raffle tickets.

The auction begins after the dining room closes. Usually the auction alternates with music played at the bandstand until all items are sold. The music and dancing continues until late into the afternoon with many people staying to socialize.

After the festa ends (usually 7 p.m.), the Brothers and Sisters meet in the main hall to select the dominga hosts for the following year. Two boxes are used. The first box contains one slip of paper for each member who wishes to be a host, with their name written on it. The second box contains an equal number of slips of paper;

seven are numbered (1 through 7) and the others have a zero. A member who was not a host this year picks the first name from the first box. That person then comes up and picks a num-

ber from the second box; if he or she is lucky, the paper will indicate which of the seven domingas he or she will host, but most pick a zero, which means he or she will not be a host in the coming year. That person then picks a name from the first box and that person goes through the same process. This continues until all seven numbers have been selected.

The first dominga host brings the crown and scepter home and keeps it on display in a prominent public place in their home until the week of the first dominga.

IDES of East Falmouth

The Third Wave (late 1960s and 70s) of Portuguese immigrants arriving in Falmouth were almost all Azoreans, with many from Terceira [52], an island just over 90 miles from São Miguel. Most of the traditions of the Fresh Pond HGS were based on those of the islands of São Miguel, Pico, and Faial as they were in the 1890s. The new immigrants were used to the traditions of Terceira in the 1960s. At first they attended the festa in Fresh Pond, but as they became more numerous and more

---

52   The second most populated Azores island and location of a United States Air Force base. It was originally named the "Island of Jesus Christ."

established, this younger group decided to host their own festa at the Skeet Club on Old Meeting House Road. The following year they formalized their group as the Irmandade de Divino Espirito Santo of East Falmouth and began holding their festa at the Fresh Pond Holy Ghost Hall the last weekend in June. The Fresh Pond Holy Ghost Society and the Irmandade do Espirito Santo of East Falmouth are mutually supportive, each helping the other, and many members of each organization attend both festas.

The founders were all from Madeira: João and Manuel Silveira (brothers), Leonel Freitas, Francisco Fernandes, and José Ourique. José moved to California in the first year and was replaced by Abel Rebello. The original five founders donated the main crown. Tony Fernandes was not a founder, but has been a member since the first festa. The founders kept their offices the first two years, but every year since then five new officers have been elected.

Three women have also contributed since the beginning: Maria Ávila, Fátima Fernandes, and Maria João Rebello.

Of this original group, Leonel, Francisco, Abel, Fátima, and Maria remain active. Leonel is the current President and Fátima and Maria are in charge of all food prepared for the festa. João and Manuel returned to the Azores, while José moved to California, and Maria is deceased.

The Fresh Pond HGS has two crowns, including one called "the small crown." The IDES, in addition to the main crown used for the domingas and the coronation, has six that are on display during Mass.

There are many other differences between the two festas, some obvious and some less so. Perhaps the most obvious difference is that the IDES has a procession that includes a marching band to bring the crown to Saint Anthony's church, a practice discontinued by the Fresh Pond HGS.

The child chosen for coronation at the IDES festa Mass is usually a little older, enough so that she gives a reading during the coronation Mass.

The IDES festa is a two-day event, usually feeding sopas free to 500 or more people. The marching band plays the Holy Ghost hymn one last time in front of the hall before the crowns are placed on the altar.

The Sopas meal itself is a little different than that served by the older group. The bread is denser and a little more sour, linguiça and other meats are also cooked in the broth, and they do not use the separator. In the beginning, the members made all of the bread at home; now they get it from the New Bedford Bakery or Economy Bakery (also in New Bedford).

The IDES also introduced family style meals, where all food is placed in the middle of the table and everyone helps himself or herself. Prior to this, the original group served individual meals, but they soon adopted the IDES practice of serving family style.

Today, the IDES has over a hundred male and female members, with most from Falmouth but others from Hyannis and New Bedford, all of who are welcome at meetings and invited to hold office. Membership dues are commonly paid but not obligatory; members are thanked each year with a gift of meat, wine, sweet bread, and homemade bread.

Holy Ghost Society of Santuit and Cotuit

The Barnstable villages of Santuit and Cotuit lie about five miles northeast of Waquoit. Cotuit is on the bay while Santuit is slightly inland. The first Portuguese immigrants to settle in these villages - Joseph B. Folger[53], George and John Williams, and Joseph Snow - were from the Azores.

Unlike Falmouth, where most Azoreans were from São Miguel, the Cotuit and Santuit settlers were from Faial. They were all whaling ship seamen who jumped ship and swam to shore in 1836, becoming some of the earliest Portuguese immigrants in the country, slightly preceding the first wave[54] of immigration.

---

53   All of the four immigrants adopted American surnames. Folger's real surname was Bettencourt. He took the name Folger from the Captain of the whaling ship he abandoned. Snow's real surname was Neves, which translates to Snow in English. Their original Portuguese surname of the Williams brothers is unknown.

54   The first wave of immigration, whaleboat seamen, is generally regarded as the period from 1840 to 1870.

For over 60 years they were the only Portuguese immigrants in the Santuit area. Eventually Joseph Snow moved to

Hyannis and became a fisherman, the Williams brothers moved to Osterville, and Joseph Folger stayed in Santuit where he later purchased the cranberry bogs he worked in as a laborer.

As happened in Falmouth, Portuguese immigrants[55] from the second wave of immigration[56] settled here between 1889 and 1910. These immigrants included the families of Frank Frazier, John Enos Frazier, Antone Cabral Matias, Jr., Antone Matias, Antone C. Medeiros, Manuel C. Medeiros, John Rapoza, the Rebello brothers Joseph and Antone, Jack Rogers, John Rego Souza, and John Souza. Many of these immigrants were employed at the Folger cranberry bogs.

The first Portuguese immigrants to practice Catholicism actively in Santuit were Antone and Jacqueline Matias, who settled there in the 1890s. The closest Catholic Church at the time was St. Joseph's in Woods Hole, sixteen miles away. Jacqueline Matias built a small altar in the front room of their home, with a statue of the Virgin Mary on the left side, a statue of St. Joseph on the right, and the Crown

55   Including the families of Antone Cabral Matias Jr., Antone and Jacqueline Mathias Sr., Frank Frazier, John Rogers, Jack Rogers, John Rego Souza, John Repoza, brothers Joseph and Antone Rebello, Manuel C. Medeiros, Antone C. Medeiros, John Souza, John Duarte, and John Enos Frazier.

56   The American Expansion wave is generally regarded as the period from 1870 to 1920.

of the Holy Ghost in the center. She held religious services for adults and Sunday school classes for the children.

St. Francis Xavier church was established in Hyannis in 1902, and the then mission chapel Our Lady of the Assumption in Osterville was established in 1905. The chapel was enlarged in 1916, and again in 1926. Finally, in 1928 Bishop Daniel Feehan established it as a parish. In 1938,[57] the St. Jude chapel was built next to the Matias homestead for the Catholics in Santuit.

The founding of the Holy Ghost Society of Santuit and Cotuit probably dates back to May 17, 1891, the Pentecost Sunday when Jacqueline invited five Catholic families to celebrate the feast. This would make it perhaps the earliest

57   The same year the stone arch was built in front of the Fresh Pond Holy Ghost Society hall.

such society in America. The original crown, brought to Santuit by Antone and Jacqueline, was made of tin. Her prayer that it might someday be plated with silver was never realized, but the Santuit society continues to this day, attracting celebrants from all over the country.

The Holy Ghost Today in the Azores

Azoreans are intensely religious Roman Catholics, with a deep religious sentiment that goes beyond the Church. It has been said that above all, in the Azores there is religion. It is as much a part of their daily life as the air they breathe. Their profound beliefs find expression in the many festas on religious holidays. The single largest one is the Festa do Senhor Santo Cristo dos Millagres (Christ of Miracles) held on the fifth Sunday after Easter in Ponta Delgarda, but by far the most common and most popular are the many Festa do Divino Espirito Santos.

Just as Catholicism began in Jerusalem and is today centered in the Vatican, so has the Azores become the epicenter of the Festa do Divino Espirito Santo. It is celebrated in every town on every island with minor variations, often around special small buildings called Impérios built specifically for that purpose. It is a living folk tradition that has differences from island to island, and even from town to town.

The festa is the culmination of an annual cycle that begins with the selection of hosts for the seven domingas and ends with a coronation and a procession to a festa where sopas is served free to all.

The cycle classically begins on Trinity Sunday with the election of the religious "emperor" of the festa and the selection of hosts for the seven domingas. It ends 51 weeks later on Pentecost Sunday with distribution of sopas free to anyone who shows up.

The "emperor" has a symbolic role; he is either chosen from the mordemos (men organizing the event) or a young boy sponsored by them. The emperor receives the crown and scepter on Trinity Sunday and brings them to his home until the first dominga.

The trinchante is the decision-maker; he sets up and coordinates all activities to prepare for and conduct the festa.

Throughout the year people in the village both donate to and help prepare for the festa. During the harvest and winemaking seasons, women and girls carry a decorated basket through the community collecting donations to the Holy Ghost.

Domingas start the week after Easter. The crown is displayed on an altar in the host's home, where people are welcome to pray and share refreshments. In many villages the rosary is said every day in the host's home. On Saturday, the crown and scepter are moved to the next host's home.

Some women start baking cakes two weeks before the festa, but the bread baking usually begins on Pentecost Wednesday.

Pentecost Thursday (sometimes Friday) is the festa do bezerro (festival of the calves). The calves that will provide the meat are brought from the fields, decorated with flowers, ribbons, and bells, and paraded through the streets, followed by the trinchante, dominga hosts, mordemos, relatives, guests, musicians, and singers.

After the calves are butchered, the meat and bread for the festa are displayed at the emperor's house, where a priest blesses them.

On Pentecost Saturday, a procession with a band and most of the community brings the food to the império, a small chapel or building built exclusively for this purpose.

Alms (meat, bread, and wine blessed by the priest) are given to the poor and to members of the brotherhood. Pentecost Sunday begins with free distribution of sopa da manhã (soup of the morning) and preparation of the Pentecost meal. After this a procession led by the flag of the Holy Spirit goes to the Church, followed by the person to be crowned, her attendants carrying the crown and scepter, and young girls dressed in white (to symbolize purity). Sometimes there are foliões, members in traditional clothing who sing and play music, followed by the band at the end of the procession.

The priest waits for the procession at the church door, where he blesses the crowns and the people. The crowns are placed on the altar and the Mass begins. The coronation takes place immediately following the Mass, followed by a procession to the teatra, where the community meal of sopas do Espirito Santo (soup made from boiled meat and cabbage) and wine is served for free.

At the end of the day, when all the food has been eaten, the crown is returned to the emperor's house, where it is displayed for three days.

On Trinity Sunday, the cycle begins again.

IMPÉRIOS

The impérios dot the Azorean landscape, testifying to the popularity and intense emotions surrounding the Festa do Divino Espirito Santo. The sheer number of them is staggering: there are about 50 on Terceira[58], an island of less than 150 square miles. If they were evenly distributed, they would be less than two miles apart; in a town the size of Falmouth, there would be fifteen impérios.

These colorful chapels stand in sharp contrast to the whitewashed residences and public buildings of brick, stone, or concrete. They are unusually ornate with multiple architectural elements, often with a white dove or crown at the top of the facade.

Many impérios have another building attached for storing the meat, bread, and wine used for the festa as well as flags and other items used in the celebration.

Most of the impérios are masonry buildings dating back to the nineteenth and early twentieth centuries, often sponsored by immigrants. They replaced the original wooden buildings, many of which were temporary.

---

58   Some large parishes have three or more.

VARIATIONS

While there is much consistency among the Holy Ghost feasts there are also some significant differences:

- With each community hosting its own festa, there are so many that some groups coordinate with each other so they are on different Sundays throughout the summer months.
- The symbolic role of "emperor" is usually male, based on the tradition that Queen Elizabeth so honored the poorest man in the kingdom. However, in many festas a young girl is crowned "Queen," honoring the founder of this tradition.
- The império and teatra are not always different buildings.
- Most, but not all, festas are two day events.
- The Holy Ghost is sometimes invoked for catastrophic events, like volcanic eruptions, earthquakes and even serious personal illness, where people carry the crowns to the churches and pray. In some instances the procession is to the location of the catastrophe. Sometimes a special festa celebrates their answered prayers.
- In some communities, the procession to dominga homes includes flags and other items used to celebrate and honor the Holy Ghost.
- The altar used to display the crown during domingas is usually wooden, covered with a white tablecloth, and decorated with flowers.
- Some festas — especially on Terceira — include alcatra (slow roasted beef, smoked bacon, onions and spices marinated in wine) with the Pentecost meal.

Perspectives on the Future

Falmouth today is a diverse eclectic community where artists, scientists, professionals, businessmen, millionaires, tradesman, and laborers mingle. As in most of America, with increased understanding, insular diversity and prejudice has increased levels of acceptance, mutual appreciation, and respect. People of all ethnicities are welcome at the festa, and more and more of them attend.

Transportation and communication improvements in the last 130 years have increased the diaspora of all ethnic groups, including the Portuguese. Descendants of the founding families and early members are now spread across America and beyond. The festa is for many an annual reunion, and so refreshing old family ties and renewing friendships increase the inherent joy of the folk celebration. It remains a unique event enjoyed by people of all ages.

Much has changed over the years, but the essence of a living tradition that was over five centuries old when Americans won their war of independence from Great Britain continues.

As long as I can remember, as generations evolve and cultures mix, people have worried about the future of the festa. I have stopped doing so and enjoy its authenticity, passing it along to others, rather than speculate on outcomes.

Postscript

Answering questions raised by old Francisco's "go back to what?" comment led to more than a few surprises. None of these were greater than unearthing common roots.

I was aware at a very young age that my great-grandparents were immigrants, and that there were differences between the Portuguese immigrants and the Yankees who had been in Falmouth for centuries.

The Pilgrims and Puritans and other immigrants - commonly referred to as "colonists" - came to this country to escape the religious oppression in England. They were attracted to a new world where the local population had been decimated[59]. Having escaped religious intolerance, as they developed settlements they themselves in turn practiced intolerance with those who disagreed with them: the founders of Sucannesset, later renamed Falmouth, were Quaker sympathizers who were not tolerated in Barnstable. And so, in a sense, they were outcasts of outcasts.

---

[59]   the original Plymouth settlement was in fact built on the site of an Indian town abandoned because of illnesses brought by Europeans visiting the area

In the fifteenth century the unpopulated Azores and Cape Verde islands were in effect the first "New World". They were colonized by immigrants at the end of the Middle Ages seeking relief from continuous warfare and starvation. Centuries later, some of their descendants would emigrate to America. In a sense, they were immigrants of immigrants.

Outcasts from outcasts founded Falmouth as it grew and prospered for almost two centuries before farms and industry began failing. The arrival of immigrants of immigrants fueled the cranberry bogs and strawberry farms that made Falmouth again prosperous for decades while the tourism industry rooted and flourished. Today, outcasts and immigrants are the backbone of the infrastructure that is Falmouth.

In writing this book, I came to learn that although there were differences between the Yankee colonizers and the Portuguese immigrants, some of them came from common roots taking different paths over many generations to end up at the same place. Before colonizing America became a real option, people in England suffered from increasing ebbs and flows of waves of religious oppression washing England. Some of them went to the Azores, and these included the ancestors of Manuel Viera Martins — one of the founders of the Fresh Pond Holy Ghost Association.

✾ ✾ ✾

It's easy to think only of today's unsolved problems and to forget those our predecessors dealt with. Many years

ago I read a poem[60] that seemed uniquely appropriate for
Portuguese-American immigrants, and later found it was
actually written about Sephardic Jews outcast first from
Spain and later from Portugal. It is very appropriate for
closing this book:

A feeling of joy descends slowly
Finding its resting place within me
The images of the past now an inspiration.

I have survived, I am here, I am alive
Connected always to my past
with love and saudade
For those who went before.

I now face the future
With the wholeness of spirit
that is victorious.

---

60   by Rufina Bernardetti Silva Mausenbaum. See http://www.saudades.org/

APPENDICES

ABOUT THE HOLY GHOST

The phrase Holy Ghost, or Holy Spirit, refers to the Holy Trinity, one of the most fascinating - and controversial - Christian dogmas[61].

The Holy Trinity is a mystery of the Roman Catholic Church. In this sense, mystery does not mean a riddle, but rather a reality that we may begin to grasp intellectually but ultimately must know through faith. It means that God is one in essence (Greek ousia), but distinct in the identities of the Father, the Son, and the Holy Spirit, remaining united in will and essence.

The Son is said to be eternally begotten of the Father, while the Holy Spirit is said to proceed from the Father through the Son. Each member of the Trinity interpenetrates one another, and each has distinct roles in creation and redemption.

---

61   this section copied from http://www.churchyear.net/trinitysunday.html

Trinitarianism – the Trinity doctrine – has been the subject of much spirited discussion. The term itself came into popular use in the second century and was codified by a council of bishops in AD 325 in Nicaea, hence the name, Nicene Creed. In the latter half of the fourth century the Roman Catholic Church dealt with those who specifically denied the divinity of the Holy Spirit, by adding more text to the creed.

ABOUT PENTECOST SUNDAY

Pentecost Sunday is one of the three major feasts of the Roman Catholic Church, second only to Easter Sunday and Christmas. Pentecost Sunday, celebrated 50 days after Easter, commemorates the descent of the Holy Spirit on the Apostles.

The Acts of the Apostles recounts the story of the original Pentecost when Jews gathered in Jerusalem to celebrate the Jewish feast[62]. On that Sunday, ten days after our Lord's Ascension, the eleven Apostles (Judas had committed suicide) and the Virgin Mary were gathered in the Upper Room, where they had seen Christ after His Resurrection:

"And suddenly there came a sound from heaven, as of a mighty wind coming, and it filled the whole house where they were sitting. And there appeared to them parted tongues as it were of fire, and it sat upon every one of them: And they were all filled with the Holy Ghost, and they began to speak with divers tongues, according as the Holy Ghost gave them to speak."

[Acts 2:2-4]

On that day, the Apostles were given the gifts of the Spirit and began preaching the gospel in the languages that the Jews gathered there spoke. About 3,000 people were converted and baptized that day. Pentecost is often called "the birthday of the Church" because the descent of the Holy Spirit completes Christ's mission.

In years past, Pentecost was celebrated with greater solemnity than it is today. In fact, the entire period between

---

62   It supplants the Jewish Pentecost, celebrated fifty days after Passover, which commemorates the sealing of the Old Covenant on Mount Sinai.

Easter and Pentecost Sunday was known as Pentecost (and it still is called Pentecost in the Eastern churches, both Catholic and Orthodox). During those 50 days, both fasting and kneeling were strictly forbidden, because this period was supposed to give us a foretaste of the life of Heaven.

FOUNDING FAMILIES

The founding families were all Azoreans, emigrating from São Miguel, Pico, Fayal, and São Jorge. All but one were born in the Azores: Manuel G. Souza was born in Rhode Island of Azorean parents. Early members included Cape Verdeans[63], most notably Louis Santos[64].

Three of the founding families were named Souza, but they are unrelated. There were two sets of siblings:

1. Francisco Teixeira and his sister Maria Rosa Teixeira, who married Joseph Sylvia White in São Miguel. Joseph and Maria immigrated in 1895; Francisco followed five years later.
2. Sisters Maria Josefa Martin (wife of Manuel Viera Martin) and Evarista Sylvester (wife of Joseph Sylvester). Maria Josefa immigrated with her husband in 1883; Evarista is believed to have immigrated about 1878 by herself.

FAMILY SUMMARIES

de Andrade, Jose Silveira, aka Joe Andrews and Tio Carassa. Born April 2, 1853, on Fayal island in the Azores and immigrated in 1889. He married Philomena de Gloria Goulart in 1879; she was born on October 2, 1855 on Fayal, Azores. Their

---

63 Manuel Morris, aka "Snowball", was a regular participant but never formalized his membership.

64 Louis Santos was born about 1881 (1920 Census, Roll T625_679, Page 1A, Enumeration District 12) and immigrated in 1890. He married Mary Santos, born about 1892, immigrating in 1907. Children: Robert (1902), Louis (1913), Barvinita (1904), and Aurora (1906)

children were: Olinda "Nellie"(1882), Anna Marie (1898), Mary (1880), Sarah (1884), Eleanore (1885), Olinda (1888), Manuel (1890), Rosella (1893), Frank (1892), Joseph Jr (1896), and (unnamed) infant. Joe was a farmer.

Brown, Anthony. Born January 1880 in the Azores and immigrated in 1897. In 1900 he was identified in the census as a boarder with the Manuel Enos family and his occupation was listed as a laborer[65]. Marital status unknown; presumed single.

Cunha, Manuel. Born about 1860 in Portugal, assumed Azores but not verified; He immigrated in 1901. Manuel married Mary Cunha about 1899. Mary was born in 1863. Their children were: John (1900), Louis (1901). All four immigrated in 1901. Manuel died between 1910 and 1920, and his family moved from Barnstable to Falmouth[66,67].

Dutra, Manuel. Born August 1856 on Fayal island in the Azores and immigrated in 1875, possibly on Brig Para disembarking in Boston. He married Mary J. Dutra in 1882. Children: Mary (1888), Jessie (1889).

Martins, Manuel Viera, aka Manny Martin and Tio Calhau. Manuel was born April 12, 1843 in the town of Lajes on Pico Island in the Azores. He married Maria Josefa Rodrigues Gonçalves in 1878; she was born 1853 in the town of Candelaria on Pico

---

65   1900 United States Census; Falmouth, Barnstable, Massachusetts; Roll T623_631, page 6A, Enumeration District 9.

66   1910 Census: Barnstable, Barnstable, Massachusetts: Roll T624_571, Page 24, Enumeration District1

67   1920 Census: Falmouth, Barnstable, Massachusetts: Roll T626_679, Page 3B, Enumeration District 12

Island in the Azores. They immigrated in 1883.
Their children were: Mary Martin (May 29,1883),
Manuel Martin, Jr. (February 1, 1887). Tio Calhau
was initially a whaler and later a farmer.

Da Rosa, Francisco Perry, aka Francisco Perry Rose. Born
1848 on Pico Island in the Azores. Married Mary
Ann (also from Pico) bef. 1882. Children: Mary,
Frank, Anthony, John (1880), Joseph (1884), and
Manuel (1886). After Mary Ann's death in 1889 he
married widow Antonia George Souza (born 1853).
Their children: Clara A. (1891), Fred (1893), Carl
(189x), and Amelia (1900).

Souza, Antone. Born 1888 on Terceira Island in the
Azores. Immigrated 1892 at Ellis Island on the
cargo ship Oevenum. Married Mary Coelho about
1909; she was, born in 1888 on São Jorge, Azores,
immigrated 1889. Married about 1909. Children:
Carl (1910), Mary (1916), Elsie (1920), Antone
(1922).

Souza, John. Born 1890 in the Azores, immigrated 1902.
Married Mary Souza about 1915; she immigrated
in 1909.

Souza, Manuel Grudeen. Born about 1888 in Rhode
Island. Spouse: Martina Souza, born in the Azores.
Married about 1910. Their children: Mary (1913),
Manuel (1914), Albert (1915), Amelia (1916),
John (1912), Jesse (1923), Louise (1925), and
George (1929).

Sylvester, Joseph. Born 5/23/1871 in the town of Fenais
da Ajuda on São Miguel island in the Azores;
immigrated 1887 on the ship Benguella in
Providence. Married Evarista Rodrigues Gonçalves

in 1893; she was born 10/15/1866 in the town of Candelaria on Pico island in the Azores, and probably immigrated in 1878. Children: Mary Sylvester (4/1/1903).

Teixeira, Francisco. Born Feb 27, 1871 in the town of Achada on São Miguel island in the Azores. Married Maria T. Silva on April 1, 1904. Maria was born in 1880. Children: Joseph, Mary (1/25/1905), Rose Victoria (1906), Georgiana (5/28/1907), Manuel (1908), Frank (1909), Lucinda (1910), Sophia (1913), Margarita (3/24/1915), Morris (12/3/1920), and Ernest (1922).

White, Joseph (da Silva), aka Joe White. Born Jose Silva about 1866 in the town of Achada on São Miguel island in the Azores; immigrated 1891[68]. Married Maria Rosa Teixeira who was born May 15, 1968, also in Achada. They were married 1895 at St. John's in New Bedford. Children: Manuel (September 13, 1887), Joseph Jr. (1901), Mary (1902), and Evangelina (1910).

The closeness of these founding families is underscored by subsequent marriages. As noted earlier, Joseph da Silva White married Francisco Teixeira's sister, Mary Rosa. Joseph Sylvester and Manuel Martin became in-laws when Joseph married Evarista and Manuel married her sister, Mary Josefa.

---

68   1920 United States Census; Falmouth, Barnstable, Massachusetts; Roll T625_679, Page 1A, Enumeration District 12.

Additionally, there were four first generation marriages:

1. Elsie Souza, daughter of Antone and Mary Souza, married Joseph Teixeira, son of Francisco and Maria Teixeira.
2. Mary Sylvester, daughter of Joseph and Evarista Sylvester, and niece of Manuel and Maria Josefa Martins, married Manuel S. White, son of Joseph and Maria Rosa White.
3. Olinda "Nellie" Andrews, daughter of José Silveira de Andrade and Philomena Goulart, married Joseph Rose, son of Francisco Perry and Marianne da Rosa.
4. Joseph White Jr., son of Joseph da Silva White and Mary White, married Lurith Rogers, the daughter of one of the founders of the Santuit Holy Ghost Association.

FALMOUTH TIMELINE

1600   Court of Plymouth Colony sets aside 10,500 acres
       for exclusive use of the Praying Indians of Bourne

1616   Wampanoags contract yellow fever from European
       traders. Two thirds die within three years.

1661   Settlers each awarded two parcels, one for wood and
       one for farming.

1675   Metacomet's War (aka King Phillip's War) begins;
       local Wampanoags do not formally participate.

1685   Falmouth purchases land from Native Americans
       and extends eastern border to the Childs River.

1700   Dexter mill built on Coonamesset River for grin-
       ding corn

1725   Boundary readjusted between Falmouth and
       Mashpee to include all of Waquoit to the Quashnet
       River.

1763   Mashpee Plantation established, opening settlement
       to outsiders

1767   Second gristmill on Backus River (below Mill Pond
       near East Falmouth library on what is now Rte 28)

1776   Continental Congress encourages salt production
       with a bounty of 1/3 dollar per bushel.

1787   First wind-powered gristmill

1795   Waquoit overshot mill built on Moonakis River.
       First processes corn, then wool and wood.

1820   Vessels for coastal trade built at White's Landing.
       Moonakis River dammed and Alan Green builds
       first gristmill in Waquoit

1825   Alexander Clarke ready to receive "commands for
       Carding Wool & Dressing Cloth... on the Grist and
       Saw Mill dam at the head of Wawquawetts Bay."

1830 First "wool manufacturing" built at site of Dexter's Mill.

1831 Falmouth raises more sheep than any Cape Cod town.

1831 Children help produce salt in 9,000 evaporation vats.

1832 Quashnet River dammed for Grist Mill

1832 Shingle mill (later woolen) built on east side of gristmill by Zenas Eber and Harrison Goodspeed

1834 Mashpee District established after Woodland Revolt.

1840 Quashnet River mill converted to wool, used until 1855

1841 Falmouth extends eastern border to Red Brook, encompassing both sides of the Quashnet.

1850 Glass factory (brief)

1853 26 acres of cranberry bogs

1854 Ordnance against free roaming sheep

1855 Falmouth sells 5,000 cords of wood, 40% of Cape sales.

1855 Carriage works erected in Waquoit

1858 Sometime prior to this date, people started importing flour and the Backus River mill was converted to wood.

1859-1889 Pacific Guano Company employs 150-200 men.

1859-1890 Dennison Company pays $12,000 for tag tying as home industry.

1861-1865 Falmouth mills woolen cloth for Civil War uniforms

1865 Mills must stop Sat-Mon to let herring pass

1865 Salt works in decline.

1870   Falmouth Heights developed as a resort community.

1871   Last salt works closed.[69]

1872   Railroad comes to Falmouth

1873   Panic of 1873, "The Long Depression"[70]; lasts six years.

1874   134 farms use 55% of available land[71]. About 70 acres in cranberries.

1879   Iceboxes replace spring houses, cellars, and wells

1881   Woods Holl becomes a station of the United States Fish Commission.[72]

1882   St. Joseph's Roman Catholic Church founded to serve Irish Catholics working at Pacific Guano Company.

1885   Cranberry crop is 2,234 barrels, bringing in $17,379.[73]

1890   646[74]dwelling places and 118 farms. Population 2,520 but only 695 registered voters.

1886   New Bedford, Martha's Vineyard, and Nantucket Steamship Company builds a wharf at the Heights and establishes steamboat service.

1888   Large building erected in 1888 to be used summers as a Biological Institute.

1889   Falmouth's assessed value is $4,000,000, second to none in Barnstable County[75]

1890   Mill ponds converted to cranberry bogs.

---

69   History of Barnstable County, Meyo, p. 672.

70   Nationwide, 89 of 364 railroads go bankrupt; 18,000 business fail; unemployment hits 14%. Construction halts and real estate values fall.

71   12,564 of 23,000 acres.

72   History of Barnstable County, Meyo, p. 671.

73   Nason's Massachusetts Gazetteer, 1890, pp. 302-305

74   Nason's Massachusetts Gazetteer, 1890, pp. 302-305

75   History of Barnstable County, Meyo, p. 642

1890   John Amaral (Emerald) starts to grow strawberries after noting plants growing near refuse.

1894   Quashnet River mill burns and never repaired

1894   Falmouth ships 15,000 barrels of cranberries, 1/10 of Massachusetts total

1905   343 acres of cranberry bogs, a high point for Falmouth

1908   Deacon's Pond becomes Falmouth's Inner Harbor

1912-1916   Falmouth mushroom business

1916   Coonamesset Ranch's 14,000 acres makes it the largest landholding east of the Mississippi

1920   USDA declares Falmouth the country's highest yield producer of strawberries

1921   Falmouth's Cape Cod Conserve Company cans 7,753 cans of corn. They also can apples, string beans, lima beans, and beets.

1937   Strawberry industry at peak. Falmouth grows more strawberries than any other town in the Northeast.

1937   Coonamesset Ranch shifts focus towards recreation with a polo field and an airport for tourists.

1954   Two hurricanes damage Quashnet River cranberry bogs. Operation closed.

1970   Quashnet River restoration begins. Now part of Mashpee National Wildlife Refuge

FALMOUTH, FROM BARNSTABLE TO SUCANNESSET

Pilgrims and Puritans

The Pilgrims who founded Plymouth Colony were seeking relief from religious oppression in England. Many members of their congregation were fined, removed from office, and even imprisoned in England; they left their farms for the Netherlands in 1608. They first settled in the industrial center of Leiden, where they enjoyed religious freedom but had trouble adjusting to industrial life and slowly but increasingly resented their children adopting Dutch customs and language and serving in the Dutch army. Already concerned about their cultural identify, they were alarmed when England attempted to arrest and extradite one of their leaders, William Brewster. They succeeded in finding English backers willing to provide financial backing for a venture in the new world. It is important to note that the Pilgrims were religious separatists, who sought religious satisfaction *outside* the Church of England. They believed that salvation was best attained by *individual righteousness*. Plymouth Colony struggled at first, losing half its population the first winter, but reinforcements arrived from England and the population began increasing.

A few years after the Pilgrims established Plymouth Colony, the Puritans established Massachusetts Bay Colony in the Boston - Salem area. The Puritans also had religious beliefs not accepted by the Church of England, but they thought they could achieve relief by working for religious reform *within* the Anglican Church. They believed salvation could best be achieved as a group "purifying" itself and setting an example of *collective righteousness* for the entire world.

The main differences between the Pilgrims and Puritans were (1) working within the Church and (2) individual versus collective righteousness. Both groups believed the Bible was the ultimate authority and sought change consistent with the religious reform sparked by Martin Luther. As with any movement seeking social change, there were strongly differing opinions about the amount of change required. Both groups were considered radicals.

The Great Migration of the 1630s saw 20,000 colonists arrive, most in the Boston - Salem area, greatly increasing the number of Puritans. More and more settlements developed. Sandwich, adjacent to Plymouth, was founded in 1639, as was Barnstable, adjacent to Sandwich.

Barnstable

Barnstable was founded by Reverend John Lothrop, a former pastor of a Congregational Church in London who was imprisoned for two years and banished to America upon his release. Lothrop arrived in Boston in 1634 and became pastor of the First Church in Scituate until 1639 when a dispute resulted in Lothrop and his followers founding a settlement in Barnstable.

Despite Lothrop's own imprisonment, banishment, and being forced out of his Church in Scituate, he was not sympathetic to dissenters in Barnstable. Isaac Robinson[76] was one of Rev. Lothrop's followers in 1639 Barnstable. He was an active and responsible freeman, one of the minority accorded voting privileges. In 1645, Isaac was appointed deputy to the General Court and in 1647 he negotiated a land purchase for the town from a Native American. Despite

---

76   Isaac was born ether in Amsterdam or Leiden about 1610, shipped to Boston in 1630, and lived in Plymouth before moving to Scituate.

his longstanding status and service, because Robinson came to sympathize with the Quakers in Sandwich, he was dismissed from civil employment and stricken from the list of freemen. [77]

Falmouth

In 1659, Robinson, with four other persons, was granted permission to purchase land. On March 5, 1660, additional permission was given to others to join them - including Rev. Lothropp's son. On June 4, they set sail and although they carried a letter of recommendation to the Church at Martha's Vineyard, they landed in what is now Falmouth and received permission from the court to settle there.

The original name of Falmouth is Sucannesset. The tract of land extended from Woods Hole along the sound to Five-Mile river (also known for a while as Dexter's River, and in current times as the Coonamesset River), extending northward four or five miles. In 1685, permission was granted to purchase additional land from Native Americans east of Five-Mile River, in what is now called East Falmouth. The eastern boundary of Sucannesset became Childs River, and Fresh Pond was not far from the Mashpee line.

The earliest known legal reference to the name Falmouth appears in a deed dated March 16, 1693-4, transferring land from Robert Harper to John Gifford.

---

77   By today's standards it seems almost impossible not to be a sympathizer. Kittridge's book tells the story of a woman named Priscilla Allen. Her Quaker husband was driven from town, leaving her and the children with only a cow. The marshal then took the cow, all the corn in the house, a bag of grain donated by the neighbors, and even her copper cooking kettle.

WAQUOIT, FROM MASHPEE TO FALMOUTH

When Falmouth was first settled, Waquoit was part of Mashpee — one of the seven "praying towns" established to encourage local Indians to convert to Christianity.

Mashpee's western boundary was the Childs River; the area between the Coonamesset and Childs rivers was part of neither Falmouth nor Mashpee. Falmouth prospered and grew, and in 1685 its eastern boundary was redefined as the Childs River.

Mashpee was declared a crown district in 1763 and Europeans were allowed to begin settling there. After the American Revolution, all previous treaties with England were regarded as null and void. Mashpee's crown district status was revoked, an overseer system was established, the reservation status reaffirmed, and local residents effectively lost all rights to self-government. Settlers began moving in.

Waquoit flourished as an agricultural, fishing, and whaling community, and its rivers were dammed to create small local mills for processing wool, wood, and grains. The first saw and gristmill was built on the Quashnet in 1793, later destroyed by fire. Around 1800, a fulling mill was built on the Child's River. In 1812, Alan Green built a Grist Mill on the Quashnet River, and twenty years later Zenas Ewer built a shingle mill on the same river. Offices and other company buildings were erected nearby. White's Landing and Peter's Wharf were built on the Childs River, a good harbor for shipbuilding and transporting goods by water. Many sea captains built their residences there, establishing local businesses when they retired. A wagon and barrel factory was built, also using Childs River waterpower.

Waquoit was booming. Mashpee, on the other hand, was not. In 1833 residents submitted resolutions to assert self-government and were promptly imprisoned when they attempted to practice it, but the following year Mashpee was approved as a self-governing district assisted by a state appointed commissioner.

In 1841, Falmouth annexed Waquoit, including all land from the Childs River to Red Brook. One writer describes this as the beginning of Waquoit's "Golden Age": it had four mills, three schools, three merchants, four farms, and nine master mariners. Shipbuilding and shipping flourished at Peter's Wharf and White's Landing, with supporting businesses nearby.

PORTUGAL IN TURMOIL: 1807-1833

In 1806, Portugal was nominally ruled by Queen Maria I, who ascended to the throne in 1777 at the age of 43. Her husband and uncle, Pedro III, had died in 1786, the same year in which her mental illness became evident[78]. Her illness became worse after her son died in 1791. In 1792 she was found mentally insane and was treated by Francis Willis, physician to King George III of England who had a similar illness[79]; the Portuguese Court refused Willis' request to transfer her to England for treatment.

Prince John, her second son, assumed the role of Regent. History suggests he was a weak monarch dominated by his wife, Queen Charlotte of Spain; they were officially married on May 8, 1785 and the marriage was consummated on January 9, 1790.

Napoleon Bonaparte initiated economic warfare with Great Britain in 1806 by imposing an embargo, demanding that all nations must honor it. Portugal had been a long time ally of Great Britain, as affirmed in the 1386 Treaty of Windsor, and they refused to honor the embargo.

At this time, the Portuguese monarchy ruled with absolute power, bound by no earthly authority — not the church, not legislatures, not the social elite — the last vestiges of the theory of divine right that was increasingly rejected, most recently by the revolutions in the United States and France a few decades earlier.

---

78   She was carried back to her living quarters in a state of delirium
79   Popularized in the 2005 movie, The Madness of King George

THE PENINSULA WAR

Napoleon, initially with the aid of the Spanish, invaded Portugal. The strongly pro-Catholic monarchy fled to Brazil, creating turmoil that would last more than 30 years. The British Navy escorted the 15,000 fleeing members of the monarchy and court to Brazil, and British General William Carr Beresford took command of joint British-Portuguese military forces. . The power vacuum left by the monarchy was filled by the military and the Freemasons, who were at best not supportive of Catholic institutions; they closed monasteries, nunneries, and Catholic schools; since there was no system of public education, literacy levels and education in general — certainly for the poor — plummeted. A year later Napoleon invaded Spain and the Spanish forces cooperated with the British and Portuguese forces. Military struggles on the mainland disproportionately took their toll on the islands, both for conscription and financial support, to minimize potential civil unrest closer to home[80].

In short, for peasants life had always been difficult, with starvation never far away and volcanoes and earthquakes always a menace. Their main solace - their faith - was under attack by the government. Wars were being fought on a distant shore by a government that sought more treasure from the islands while disproportionately conscripting their young men to fight on the mainland.

The French were defeated in 1814 but the monarchy remained in Brazil. Portugal continued to be run by the military and Freemasons while liberal ideas about the role of government, spawned by the French Revolution and

---

80   To a lesser extent this was also true of mainlanders outside Lisbon. There is an old Portuguese saying "Portugal is Lisbon - the rest is just scenery."

the new government in Spain took root in Portugal, result-ing in Portuguese Constitutionalist insurrections in Lisbon and Oporto and the liberal constitution of 1820.

THE WAR OF THE TWO BROTHERS

King Joao VI agreed to support the constitution and returned from Brazil in 1821. He left his oldest son Pedro behind in Brazil. The following year Pedro declared Brazil independent of Portugal and himself its Emperor. King Joao VI's second son, Miguel, and his wife Queen Charlotte did not support the constitution and wanted to return government to the way it was in 1807. Prince Miguel was generalissimo of the army. In 1824, alarmed by the "pestilential bevy of free-masons" and with Queen Charlotte's support, Miguel took many political prisoners and ordered a siege of the Palace of Bemposta where King Joao VI was closeted with his advisor, British General William Carr Beresford. British forces succeeded in transferring King Joao VI to the British ship HMS Windsor Castle where he ordered Miguel removed as general, released all political prisoners, exiled Miguel, and Queen Carlota thereafter sequestered at Quelez Palace. King Joao seldom visited Quelez, but on one such visit in 1826 he died in the King's Bedroom after naming their daughter Infante Isabel Maria as regent to ensure that Queen Carlota would not succeed him.

PORTUGUESE CIVIL WAR[81]

Pedro briefly became King of both Portugal and Brazil, creating problems in both countries. Pedro decided to remain in Brazil as Emperor and abdicated the Portuguese throne to his seven-year-old daughter, Maria II. He nominated his brother Pedro as Regent on condition that he marry Maria when she came of age and that the two would reign together. Pedro accepted but took a different course. He accepted the Regency, dethroned Maria before she even arrived in Portugal, and took steps to restore the monarch to its pre-constitution form, including restoring to the Catholic Church what it had lost. It took Pedro eight years to regain the Portuguese throne, and when he did he supported the constitution and took aggressive action against the Church which he viewed as supporting Miguel. Seemingly continuous warfare, with its conscription and financial demands, and attacks on the Church, left the peasants worse off than before.

END OF THE TRANSATLANTIC SLAVE TRADE[82]

The wars wreaked havoc on both the Azores and Cape Verde. While the Azores economy was based on farming and fishing, the Cape Verde economy was based on the slave trade and that began coming to an end in this same period. In 1807, the United States outlawed the importation of slaves. Great Britain also abolished the slave

---

81 Also known as the Liberal War or the Miguelite War

82 Of all the abominable aspects of slavery, in terms of the number of people subjected to sheer brutality, inhumane living conditions, and high mortality rates, the transatlantic slave trade was by far the most offensive.

trade and began patrolling the African Coast for violators. Transatlantic slave trading began declining immediately, but other nations were slow to follow suit and it continued to decline for another 50 years. While both the Azores and Cape Verde suffered from the loss of young men, financial drain, and government religious infringement, Cape Verde uniquely experienced even more economic decline eliminating this immoral business as fewer slave trading ships called for resupply, repair, and shore leave.

SEISMIC ROOTS OF THE THIRD WAVE

The Immigration Restriction Act of 1921 limited immigration to 3% of each country's immigrants counted in the 1910 census, effectively all but shutting down Portuguese immigration. These restrictions remained in place until a year of violent earthquakes, volcanic eruptions, and lava flows devastated Fayal.

Hundred of earthquakes (Richter scale 5 or higher) occurred on September 27 and 28, 1957 off the western shore of Fayal. Underwater volcanic eruptions soon created one small island, then a second one. The underwater volcano became a land volcano. Lava flows followed the eruptions, linking the new land to Fayal. On May 17 1958, a major earthquake struck, completely destroying many homes and damaging several others. By the time it was all over on October 24, 1958, Fayal's land area had been expanded by almost a square mile. Hundreds of houses were destroyed, much of the island was covered in ash, and for some periods it seemed as if almost the entire island was uninhabitable. Local economies plummeted. Thousands fled the island.

The Azorean Refugee Act of 1958 opened the immigration gates. It also triggered a reexamination of immigration policy, resulting in the Immigration and Nationality Act of 1965 which abolished the national origins formula.

Immigrants were primarily motivated by economic opportunity. The monarchy had been deposed in 1910 and replaced by the corrupt First Republic which suppressed religion. The Second Republic took over in 1926, and Dictator Salazar came into power in 1933 with the Third Republic. Portugal enjoyed twenty-five years of relative stability before the seismic devastation of 1957. Between 1960 and 1980, buoyed by a booming economy, over 175,000 Azoreans immigrated to America.

It had taken Ti Calhau over three years to reach America on the whaling bark Kathleen. Those who could later find direct passage on sailing ships could do it in three to five weeks. The arrival of steamships cut this to twelve days, and then nine. By 1958 airplanes made it possible in five hours.

BIBLIOGRAPHY

"Azorean and New England Whaling and Fishing", Robert L. Santos, California State University, Stanislaus

"Book of Falmouth", 1986, Mary Lou Smith, Falmouth Historical Commission

"Cape Cod, Its People and Their History", Henry C. Kittredge, 1968, Houghton Mifflin Company.

"A Description of the Azores or Western Islands", Anonymous, Bodleian Library, assumed middle nineteenth century

"The Founding of New England", James Truslow Adams, 1921, Boston, Atlantic Monthly Press

Fourth Annual Report, [Massachusetts] Board of Railroad Commissioners, July, 1873.

"A History of the Azores Islands", James H. Guill, Golden Shield Publications, Tulare, California, 1993

"History of Barnstable County", Simeon L. Deyo, H.W. Blake & Co., 1890.

"Holy Ghost Festival", United States Air Force Fact Sheet, http://www.lajes.af.mil/library/factsheets

"The Holy Ghost Society of Santuit and Cotuit", John D. Medeiros, Holy Ghost Society of Santuit and Cotuit Centennial Souvenir, 1991.

"The Imperio in the Azores: The Five Senses in Rituals to the Holy Spirit", Maria Santa Montez[83], Traditiones, 2007, pp. 169-176.

"Our Old Waquoit House", Frederick V. Lawrence Jr, Falmouth Historical Society, 2009

---

[83]   Prof. Maria Sata Vieiera Montez, Instituto de Sociologia e Etnologia das Religioes, Universidade Nova de Lisboa, Lisboa.

"The 1858 Map of Cape Cod, Martha's Vineyard, and Nantucket", Henry F. Walling, On Cape Publications, 2009

"In Pursuit of Their Dreams: A history of Azorean Immigration to the United States", Jerry R. Williams, Center for Portuguese Studies and Culture, University of Massachusetts Dartmouth, 2003; 2nd Edition, 2007.

Journals of the Waquoit Holy Ghost Society, 1924-2010

"Pilgrim and Puritan: A Delicate Distinction", Richard Howland Maxwell, Pilgrim Society Note, Series Two, March 2003

"The Portuguese Amongst Us", John D. Medeiros, Historical Society of Santuit and Cotuit, 1979

"So Ends This Day: The Portuguese in American Whaling, 1765-1927", Donald Warrin, Center for Portuguese Studies and Culture, University of Massachusetts Dartmouth, 2010

"The Transportation Revolution and Transatlantic Migration, 1850-1914", Drew Keeling, University of California, Berkeley, 1998

US Census Records, 1880, Falmouth, Massachusetts, Pages 1-55, Supervisor District 60, Enumeration District 4.

US Census Records, 1900, Falmouth, Massachusetts, Sheets 31, Supervisor District X, Enumeration District 9

US Census Records, 1920

US Census Records, 1930

RECIPES FOR THE HOME

These recipes are for foods served in the Fresh Pond Holy Ghost Society dining room and concession stand during the 2010 and 2011 festas. They are generally "family sized" and in some cases, adapted for home cooking methods. Most have Azorean roots and evolved in America in immigrant homes that used stoves as a source of heat, where simmering and baking were natural and economical choices. Phrases like "more or less," "a little," and "until done," are frequently used by most experienced Portuguese cooks. Try these recipes and adapt them to your own taste.

SOPAS

Here's a recipe that's good for four people[84].
Ingredients
    2 lb. beef roast
    1/3 cup pickling spice
    1 1/2 heads cabbage
    6 medium onions
    12 sprigs hortelãu (mint may be substituted)
    1 tbsp salt
    2 loaves Portuguese bread

Directions
1. Cut bread into 1 1/2" slices and put on a tray so it can dry out while everything else is cooking.
2. Using cheesecloth, make a ball of the pickling spices.
3. Trim most of the fat from the roast.

---

84   The first time I asked how to cook Sopas, I was told it was easy: "take one cow....."

4. Put meat, 2 onions, pickling spice, and two 1/4 heads cabbage in the crock-pot.
5. Fill the crock-pot with water, leaving about 2" of space at the top for it to simmer without spilling over.
6. Put crock-pot on high heat until broth begins to simmer.
7. Lower heat and let simmer for at least five hours.
8. Remove ball of pickling spice, onions, and cabbage. Discard the onions and cabbage (they have flavored the broth but have absorbed too much fat). Place crock-pot on a non-heated surface for a few minutes and remove most of the fat floating on top of the broth.
9. Place crock-pot back on high heat and add the salt, 4 1/4 heads of cabbage, and 4 onions. When broth is starting to boil, lower heat to a simmer and cook for an additional 30 minutes.
10. Put half of the bread in a large metal pan and lay 6 sprigs of mint on top. Add the remaining bread and the remaining sprigs.
11. Place the meat, onions, and cabbage on a large serving platter. Pour the broth over the bread and mint, adding slightly more broth than the bread can absorb.
12. Place platter and pan on table and serve family style; or make large soup bowls with the bread, meat, cabbage, and onions.

Variations

This recipe is close to what is served at the Fresh Pond Festa by the original founders. The "greenhorns" (aka "newcomers," Third Wave) add chicken, do not remove the fat, and use white Portuguese corn bread; you might want to try it with chouriço, a spicy Portuguese sausage, or bay leafs, but try the authentic recipe before you experiment.

KALE SOUP

There are many recipes for kale soup, some with kale coarsely copped and some finely shredded, some with red beans and some without, some starting with dried split peas and others starting with pea soup, some with potatoes and/or pasta, some not, and so on and so forth. After many lively discussions, it finally dawned on me that the very best kale soup would always be the one your grandmother made when she still walked the earth. Unfortunately, they usually didn't measure anything much less write it down. This is a recipe that reminds me of the kale soup my grandmothers made.

Ingredients:
  1/2 lb. split peas
  1/2 package linguiça
  beef shank bone with meat
  salt
  2 bunches kale
  6 potatoes, peeled and cubed about 3/4"

Directions:
1. Put split peas in panella and cover with water. Allow to stand overnight.
2. Rinse peas, cover with water, bring to a boil, then simmer until peas are soft (mushy, not al dente)
3. Add linguiça and beef shank. Cover with water. Simmer until met falls from the shank bone.
4. Remove shank bone, trim fat. Discard bone and fat. Return meat to the panella.
5. Wash kale, chop, and add to panella. Ad water to cover. Simmer until kale is tender, a minimum of two hours.

FAVAS

Ingredients:
    2 lb. fava beans (dry)
    1 cup vegetable oil
    1 bunch parsley
    4 large onions
    dry red pepper
    salt

Directions:
1. Soak fava beans in cold water for 24 hours in covered pan.
2. Drain water and add fresh water to cover the fava beans. Bring to a boil and simmer until favas are tender.
3. Slice onions. Chop parley. Add onion, parsley, and vegetable oil.
4. Mix all ingredients. Add salt and dry red pepper to taste.

FEIJOADA

Ingredients:
    6 cans of white beans
    1 package of linguiça
    1/2 pound bacon
    1 large onion
    3 garlic cloves
    3 tbsp tomato paste
    2 tbsp crushed red pepper (wet)
    1/4 cup white wine
    1 cup water

Directions:
1. Chop linguiça and bacon.
2. Sauté all ingredients in 1 tbsp olive oil
3. Add water. Continue cooking until linguiça and bacon are done.
4. Add beans. Bring to a boil, then simmer until beans are tender until done.

PORTUGUESE RICE

Ingredients:
    2 - 2 1/2 cups rice
    4 - 5 cups chicken broth
    1 package linguiça, sliced into chunks.
    1 large onion, chopped.
    3 tbsp butter
    1 tbsp crushed red pepper (wet)
    2 packages Goya seasoning (with Azafran)

Directions:
1. In a saucepan add oil and butter. Heat until melted. Add onion and cook until translucent.
2. Add red pepper and linguiça. Stir. Cook 3 minutes.
3. Add chicken stock and rice. Cook on medium heat until rice is almost dry.

BACALHAU

Ingredients:
    1 lb. salted boneless codfish
    2 lb. potatoes
    2 large onions
    4 garlic cloves
    1 bunch parsley
    1/4 cup olive oil
    1/4 cup white wine
    2 tbsp tomato paste
    1 package Goya Sazonador
    1 tbsp crushed red pepper (wet)
    6 eggs
    sliced black olives

Directions:
1. Soak codfish in cold water overnight. Drain and cook codfish in cold water for 10 minutes.
2. Preheat oven to 400 degrees.
3. Boil eggs.
4. Sauté onions and garlic in the olive oil until the onions are translucent. Add parsley, white wine, tomatoes paste, and seasonings. Stir and cook 1 minute.
5. Slice potatoes and layer in the bottom of a large Pyrex baking dish. Shred codfish and layer on top of the potatoes. Cover with the sautéed ingredients.
6. Place in oven and cook until potatoes are done. Remove and allow to cool.
7. Layer sliced eggs on top and garnish with black olives.

CARNE GUISADA

Ingredients:
    2 - 3 lb. beef cubes
    6 potatoes, cut into cubes
    2 tbsp tomato paste
    1 large onion, chopped
    2 cloves garlic, minced
    1 bay leaf
    2 tbsp crushed red pepper (wet)
    1/2 cup white wine.
    salt & pepper

Directions:
1. Sauté meat and all other ingredients in sauce pan except potatoes.
2. Cover with water and cook one hour on medium heat.
3. Add potatoes. Cook until potatoes are tender.

Bom Apetit !
(Enjoy your meal!)

PRAYERS OF BLESSING[85]

Blessing of the Bread
The bread that we bless has been taken from many grains of wheat, they have been mixed together to form these loaves of bread. As we share this bread, may we also become one.
WE ASK THIS THROUGH CHRIST OUR LORD. AMEN.

Blessing of the Wine
The wine that we bless has been taken from many grapes which have been crushed together and bottled to raise our spirits. As we share this wine, may we also share the joy of life.
WE ASK THIS THROUGH CHRIST OUR LORD. AMEN.

Blessing of the Meat
Father of all goodness, our ancestors in ancient times prepared meat for your Passover Supper. In our own time we prepare this meat for this annual Portuguese Festival, bless this meat in your honor. May this food be gratifying, giving us strength that we may be a people who seek to do your will.
WE ASK THIS THROUGH CHRIST OUR LORD. AMEN.

Blessing of the Spices
In times long past, your people preserved the food that you had given with salt and spices. We ask that these spices flavor and season these foods, and our lives to your service.
WE ASK THIS THROUGH CHRIST OUR LORD. AMEN.

---

85   As said by Father Costello on May 23, 2010

Blessing of Hearts
God Our Loving Father, we ask you to bless our hearts. May we remain grateful for the ancient traditions and gifts of families. May we honor our heritage by our faithfulness to You our God, by devotion to our family and friends. May our hearts be always loving.
WE ASK THIS THROUGH CHRIST OUR LORD. AMEN.

Blessing of Hands
Lord, you supply us with all these things that we need. We ask you now to bless the hands that prepare this feast and cook this food. We ask you to keep them safe from harm. May our hands work together for your glory.
WE ASK THIS THROUGH CHRIST OUR LORD. AMEN.

BLESSED ARE YOU LORD GOD OF ALL CREATION. YOU ARE THE CREATOR OF ALL THAT IS GOOD.

BLESS THIS FOOD, AND GRANT THAT ALL WHO PARTAKE IN THIS FESTIVAL MAY BE STRENGTHENED IN BODY AND GROW IN LOVE.

BLESS OUR LIVES THAT WE MIGHT BE NOURISHMENT FOR OTHERS, AND GRATEFUL FOR YOUR GIFTS.

BLESSED ARE YOU LORD GOD, FOREVER AND EVER.